May you always
seek the wealth of
God's power, God's plan,
and God's promises!

Jammie Bonds

Matthew 6:31

Praise for Jennifer's Books

"Jennifer reminds us that finding the answers is not nearly as important as finding The Answer."

~Joni Eareckson Tada, bestselling author
and Founder of Joni & Friends, International.

"Jennifer lays down a path of hope for others who face the unthinkable."

~Philip Yancey, bestselling author of *The Jesus I Never Knew*

"A personal relationship with Christ changes our view of everything in life and makes ordinary, everyday circumstances a spiritual object lesson taught by God's Holy Spirit. Jennifer has shared with us her exciting journey of growing in Christ. May the lessons she has taken to heart reach our hearts as well."

~Bestselling author Janette Oke, *Love Comes Softly*

"Jennifer encourages all readers to believe that God has a purpose for them and that He is walking with them even through life's trials."

~*Christian Retailing* magazine

"If Jennifer dares to suggest that God had a purpose for what happened in her life, then we should listen. If she can find hope in her circumstances, then we can find hope in ours. The question is not—will tragedy come into our lives? The question is—where will we find peace, hope, and the will to go on when it does?"

~Steve Saint, author of *End of the Spear*,
son of missionary Nate Saint

"Jennifer's new book, *A Treasured Faith*, is just that... a treasure. What an incredibly readable, uplifting, convicting, and valuable jewel it is. This book offers answers to one of the most difficult challenges to our faith in such a beautiful and gracious way. It is a wonderful apologetic for those who struggle with the problem of evil and human suffering. A must read for those who need encouragement, hope, or just a reminder of how big our God really is."

~Judy Salisbury, Christian author, speaker,
and founder of Logos Presentations

A
Treasured
Faith

A Treasured Faith

Refining a Heart for the Riches of Christ

Jennifer Sands

 SAVANNAH, GA
The Olive Press

Published by The Olive Press, Savannah Georgia. Distributed by STL/Faithworks.

All biblical quotations are taken from the New American Standard Bible unless otherwise noted. Scripture taken from the NEW AMERICAN STANDARD BIBLE* unless otherwise noted, Copyright © 1960,1962,1963,1968,1971,1972,1973,1975,1977,1995 by The Lockman Foundation. Used by permission. Scripture quotations marked (NIV) are taken from the HOLY BIBLE, NEW INTERNATIONAL VERSION*. NIV*. Copyright© 1973, 1978, 1984 by International Bible Society. Used by permission of Zondervan. All rights reserved.

Feedback to the author: jennifer@jennifersands.com

Front cover photograph by Michael Gomez, courtesy of Homelife magazine. www.gomezphotography.com
Author portrait on dustjacket by Michael Angelo Travisano. www.michaelangelonj.com
Cover and interior design & layout by Pneuma Books, LLC. www.pneumabooks.com

Publisher's Cataloging-In-Publication Data
(Prepared by The Donohue Group, Inc.)

Sands, Jennifer, 1964-
  A treasured faith : refining a heart for the riches of Christ / Jennifer Sands.

  p. ; cm.

  Includes bibliographical references.
  ISBN: 978-0-9767961-3-8

1. Christian life. 2. Spiritual life--Christianity. 3. Faith. 4. Sands, Jennifer, 1964- 5. September 11 Terrorism Attacks, 2001--Religious aspects--Christianity. I. Title.

BV4501.3 .S263 2009
248.86   2009924049

PRINTED IN THE UNITED STATES OF AMERICA
on acid∞free paper
17 16 15 14 13 12 10 09   01 02 03 04 05 06 07 08

The
Olive Press

Jim & Jennifer — Thanksgiving, 1996

~

In memory of my husband, Jim

*Thank you, hon, for giving me the treasures of a
loving marriage and countless happy memories.*

*We only had six short years together,
but they are six cherished years.
You are always in my mind and in my heart,
and I will love you all the days of my life.*

~

In honor of Pastor G. Richard Fisher

*Thank you, Pastor, for being my earthly shepherd and my
spiritual mentor. For over forty years, you have given our church
the treasures of sound Bible teaching, strong leadership, and a
godly example to follow. If some words in this book are familiar
to you, it's because I take really good notes on your sermons.*

~

To my Lord and Savior Jesus Christ

*Through Whom I am redeemed and
to Whom I commit my life.
You are my strength when I am weak
You are the treasure that I seek
You are my all in all.*

Contents

For where your treasure is, there your heart will be also.

~*Matthew 6:21*

Preface

Here it is, part three of the "ATF" trilogy. (No, that does not stand for Alcohol, Tobacco, and Firearms. Nor does it stand for Automatic Transmission Fluid.) By the grace and will of God, the power of prayer, and a much-appreciated publishing team, *A Treasured Faith* joins its predecessors, *A Tempered Faith* and *A Teachable Faith*. I've said this before and I'll say it again: In those early days after losing my husband on September 11, 2001, no one could have ever convinced me that I'd be writing books. Since that tragic day, every aspect of my life has been radically changed. I went from being a very happily married pharmacist to a devastated and angry widow. After I made my peace with God, He actually made a Christian author out of me. It boggles my mind every time I think about it.

For months before I began writing this book I had been praying for God's guidance and direction as I anticipated the project. In one of my prayer journal entries from January 2007, I presented Him with this appeal: "Lord, I would really like to write again... but I don't know what to write about and with my busy schedule I'm not sure when I'll find the time to do it. So if it is Your will, please provide me with a topic and some time to put it on paper."

He addressed both of my requests in one shot.

Just two months after that journal entry, I was diagnosed with breast cancer. It was discovered by a routine mammogram with the appearance of some calcifications in my left breast. A surgical biopsy reported DCIS (Ductal Carcinoma In Situ) — aggressive, high-grade cancer cells contained within the milk ducts. It would require further surgery (a lumpectomy) followed by radiation treatments, five days a week for seven weeks.

I got the answers to my prayers (be careful what you wish for). God had indeed provided me with plenty of material — my cancer treatments — to write about, and I used those seven weeks during radiation to get started on the manuscript. Scattered throughout the pages of this book you will read about my struggle with breast cancer, but I will not dominate this book or your time with that latest development in my life. Instead I have chosen to focus on the many treasures that God has provided to us: Treasures in the form of healing. Treasures in the relationships we build. Treasures that result from our joys *and* our trials. Buried treasures that surface when we dig deep enough into our soul. Even tangible treasures that have been uncovered by archaeologists, confirming accounts in the Bible. But our greatest treasure as followers of Yeshua is our salvation through His infinite grace and His inconceivable love for us.

So put away all thoughts of 10-carat diamond rings, bars of gold recovered from shipwrecks, and billion-dollar stock market portfolios; the most precious gem is found on a cross at Calvary. The most priceless fortune is found in an empty tomb. The most valuable riches are found in the pages of the Bible. The greatest wealth is obtained through a close relationship with Jesus Christ, who says, "For where your treasure is, there your heart will be also."

·tf·

In this you greatly rejoice, even though now for a little while, if necessary, you have been distressed by various trials so that the proof of your faith, being more precious than gold which is perishable, even though tested by fire, may be found to result in praise and glory and honor at the revelation of Jesus Christ.

~1 Peter 1:6-7

14-Karat
Cancer

1

After my doctor gave me the news of my breast cancer diagnosis, I left his office in one of those surreal, autopilot states and walked to my car. My condition would require surgery followed by radiation treatments — five days a week for seven weeks. The shock of this was somewhat of a déjà vu of September 11, albeit to a much lesser degree. Like that fateful morning over five years earlier, I once again found myself repeating in my mind, *this can't be happening... this can't be happening.*

Cancer is one of those words that painfully jolts you when it's about you — just like *widow.* It gives you that sick, sinking feeling in the pit of your stomach and sends the mind racing into unfamiliar territory. *But there's no history of breast cancer in my immediate family. Maybe they're mistaken. Maybe they mixed up my biopsy with someone else's.* I suppose I didn't take the initial report of "suspicious" seriously enough. *God knows I've been through enough after 9/11... He wouldn't let this happen, too... would He?* I was stunned at the news. But then again, who expects it?

I sat alone inside my car, staring straight ahead, not ready to turn the ignition on yet. I developed an acute case of spiritual vertigo and searched for equilibrium, trying to regain my footing. My mind was still spinning in confusion, with a few meaningless reflections thrown into the mix: *Does this mean I should wear a pink ribbon now? Or is that only delegated to breast cancer survivors?* Then right on cue, my demanding, Sicilian Control Freak nature from my B.C. ("before Christ") days surfaced and I took it up with God: "Lord, I have no time in my life for breast cancer. You know how busy my schedule is. I *can't* take that much time off from work and I *can't* cancel speaking engagements." As if God might have reconsidered the whole thing, now that I made Him aware of the major flaws in His plan.

Instead, His words came into my mind and He gently reminded me, "My thoughts are not your thoughts, nor are your ways My ways (ISA. 55:8). There is an appointed time for everything... for every event under heaven (ECCL. 3:1). And besides, My grace is sufficient for you, for power is perfected in weakness (2 COR. 12:9)."

I backed down once I remembered Who I was talking to. *Okay, Lord...I'm sorry. I'll go along with Your plan...but what if...?* I still didn't completely trust His perfect plan and His perfect timing. My prognosis was good — the cancer was caught early and it had not spread beyond the milk ducts. But I still had concerns, fears, and doubts. *What if, during the surgery, the scalpel pierces the milk ducts and the cancer cells leak out into my lymph nodes? What if there are microscopic cancer cells that weren't picked up on the mammogram? What if the radiation causes even bigger problems?* What if... what if... what if... my mind was spiraling out of control, an anarchy of anxiety, and suddenly I just wanted to be held by Jim's strong arms and comforted by his familiar voice. That impossibility was even more distressing than the news of breast cancer. I could feel a downward spiral coming on. It must be stopped. Now.

I took a deep breath and reminded myself that, like September 11, God *could have* stopped this serious health issue from happening. He could have put His divine hedge of protection around me so that cancer cells could not have invaded my body. He could have. He is sovereign. He has absolute supremacy and total dominion of this universe and everything in it. Then I realized I really *was* being held by strong arms... and I *did* hear a familiar voice. They weren't Jim's and they weren't literal or audible. But they were very strong and very familiar. "I am the LORD, the God of all mankind. Is there anything too hard for me? (JER.32:27). The eternal God is a dwelling place, and underneath are His everlasting arms (DEUT. 33:27). All authority has been given to Me in heaven and on earth" (MATT. 28:18).

God *could have* stopped this attack of breast cancer, but He chose not to because He knows far more than I do about the outcome. To those who have submitted their lives to His Son, God promises that ultimately the blessings that come from trials will outweigh the pain. How do we know that? Because God says so. "The sufferings of this present time are not worthy to be compared with the glory that is to be revealed to us" (ROM. 8:18).

Yes, there was pain and deformity from my surgery and the radiation treatments were far from pleasant. You'll read more about that later. But already blessings have come from having breast cancer — including this book you are reading. Some blessings I might not see for a while, and others I may not see until eternity. But blessings will come and God's glory will be revealed.

And in case you're wondering: I am grateful to report that, as of the writing of this book, my last mammogram was clean and I am cancer free. It was diagnosed and treated within one year, thanks to God's grace, early detection, and the power of prayer. Every time I say that or write that or even *think* about that, I thank and praise God. He is the Great Physician. He is Jehovah-Rophe; He is the LORD who heals. I bow down to Him.

Having cancer can be a treasure. No, I didn't say *cancer* is a treasure. Of course not. But *having* cancer — the *experience* it-

3

self — *can be* a treasure if we allow God to use it for our good and for His glory. So I will wear a pink ribbon. Not because I want everyone to know I had breast cancer and survived it (even though I did). Not because I donate funds to the cause and support of breast cancer research (even though I do). Not because I am grateful for the many people who walked with me through this journey (even though I am). I will wear a pink ribbon because it opens up doors of opportunity to testify that God is faithful and true to every one of His promises. That's where the real treasure lies.

·tf·

Your word I have treasured in my heart, that I may not sin against you.

~Psalm 119:11

The Value of
Obedience

2

After my surgery,
the post-operative directions from my surgeon included the following: "No pushing, no pulling, no lifting, no stretching, no
bouncing, no jiggling." As my doctor recited these commands, I
visualized each prohibited activity with a red circle around it and
a red line through it — until I got to the bouncing and jiggling.
Then I burst out laughing. *No bouncing? No jiggling? I guess my
days as a belly dancer on a trampoline are over.*

"Well, do you have stairs in your home?" My doctor said, clearly
unamused by my amusement. "Then you need to secure your
breasts as you walk down the stairs so they don't bounce or jiggle."

"*Secure* my breasts?" I had a vision of a titanium undergarment, complete with a little lace bow in the center. This gave
new meaning to the Breastplate of Righteousness.

"Just cross your arms over your chest. And you must wear a
sports bra, twenty-four seven, until the incision is completely
healed."

"You want me to wear it when I *sleep?* Ugh, why not just
make me wear a straightjacket and confine me to a prison ward.
I'll be embossed with permanent indentations."

He wasn't budging, and he still had no smile. *When this is
all over, I want a trophy for enduring marathons of painfully-
tight undergarments.*

Then came even more restrictive commands from the radiation oncologist. For the duration of my seven-week radiation treatments, there would be: NO sun exposure, NO salt water, NO very hot water, NO chlorine, NO perfumes or fragrances, NO deodorants or anti-perspirants, NO soap other than unscented Dove, NO underwire bras, and absolutely NO creams or lotions other than those prescribed by the doctor. Keep in mind that my treatments were in July and August and I live at the hot and humid Jersey Shore, so any plans I had for the beach and pool were quickly terminated. The radiation treatments made my skin look and feel like a really bad sunburn... on top of a really bad sunburn... on top of a really bad sunburn. Repeat that for thirty-five sessions. Alas, I was pretty much confined to my home with very little activity. *So, I thought, I might as well start writing another book.*

Generally speaking, the results of most medical treatments depend on the compliance of the patient. There are exceptions; but for the most part, if the patient does what they're told to do, they'll have a faster recovery. Likewise, if the patient doesn't follow instructions, complications can arise and the healing process will be slower. Of course, this isn't limited to the world of health and medicine. Life works the same way, and the apostle Paul sums it up short and sweet: you reap what you sow (GAL. 6:7). Again, there are exceptions (i.e., the book of Job), but in general obedience brings forth blessings and disobedience brings forth judgment.

Well, there came a point when I couldn't stand that sports bra anymore, so I took matters into my own hands. *Enough of the straightjacket, I'm goin' for comfort. Yes, I know what the doctor said — support is important for the healing process — but he can't be right about everything. I know what's good for me.* I figured I could get just as much support from an underwire bra, so in a daring act of rebellion, I went for it.

Not too long after, a mysterious rash appeared under my breast during the radiation treatments. Upon close inspection of

8

the rash, my doctor looked me in the eye with utter shock and disdain and said, "Have *you* been wearing an *underwire* bra???" The inflection he used sounded like a suspicious father accusing his young, truant son: "Did *you cut school* today?" or like a mother confronting her guilty teenage daughter: "Did *you* take that lipstick from the store *without paying* for it?"

I had been found out. My sin had been exposed. I would now have to reap what I had sown and bear the consequence of my transgression. Not only would I have to resume wearing the dreaded sports bra again (grrr), but I was now required to apply yet another cream to the radiation burn, on top of a few other medicated creams I had earned along the way. Applying these creams and getting dressed in the morning was a major production. How I longed for the days of simply throwing clothes on and running out the door. Have you ever tried to ice a cake while it's still warm? Every spread of the knife pulls the delicate cake apart, mixing the crumbs into the icing and making a mess. That was my daily state of affairs during the summer of 2007. My doctor, the Bra Nazi, made it very clear: *No more underwire bras for you. Come back one year.*

This made me think of the story of Uzzah in 2 Samuel 6. King David ordered the ark of God to be brought to Jerusalem, and Uzzah was one of the guys responsible for moving it. God had given explicit instructions as to how the ark was to be handled — including the command that the ark could not be touched, under penalty of death. Well, Uzzah touched it, and Uzzah died. "Uzzah reached out toward the ark of God and took hold of it, for the oxen nearly upset it. And the anger of the LORD burned against Uzzah, and God struck him down there for his irreverence; and he died there by the ark of God" (2 SAM. 6:6-7).

Each time I read that story, I feel bad for Uzzah. After all, he was just trying to protect the ark from toppling over. His offense seemed so trivial and the penalty was so harsh. I mean, what

9

was so bad about touching the ark? What was so bad about wearing an underwire bra during radiation treatments? Of course, I deliberately violated my doctor's order so I deserved what I got: a painful rash, a sharp rebuke, and another layer of cream. Uzzah's intent had been honorable, but rules are rules. He still violated the Lord's clear instructions for handling the ark. And when I read that passage, one word really sticks out to me: *irreverence*.

Irreverence is at the core of every sin. It is apathy and disregard for God's instructions. It lacks fear of God's power; it lacks respect for His holiness. When I sin, it is because I simply don't care what God will think about my actions, or how He'll respond to them. *God won't mind if I tell this one little lie... after all, my intentions are sincere.* Or maybe, *God won't see or notice or mind that I'm doing this. Even if He does, He'll let me get away with it.* Or the top-of-the-charts Christian classic, *God will forgive me for it anyway.* Often I'm not even consciously aware of these foolish thought processes; but they're definitely there, deeply imbedded in my DNA.

Reverence for God. Fear of the LORD. Respect. Honor. Worshipful wonder. The word in Hebrew is *Yi'rah*. It's that spine-tingling, heart-pounding awe when I become aware of God's power. It's a positive kind of fear when I realize I'm in the presence of the Almighty. *Yi'rah* should make me dread God's disapproval of my sin — not only because I dread the consequences, but because I adore Him and therefore I should want to live in obedience to Him.

I had irreverence for my doctor when I wore the underwire bra. Again, was it a big deal? No. But the fact of the matter is that I went against his clear instructions, and I paid the price. *He won't see or notice or mind that I'm doing this. And even if he does, he'll let me get away with it.* True, he never saw the actual bra, but he sure saw the result of the bra. The rash disclosed what was in my heart: *I do not respect your authority or your expertise and I'm going to do what I want.* And unfortunately, those are the exact same sentiments that I'm conveying to my precious Lord and Savior when I go against His Word.

I'm always amazed at how God corrects and teaches me and what He uses to get His point across. In the past He has used everything from dogs to spiders to closets to computers to mattresses to scuba diving equipment. You may have read about those lessons in my other books, and now you and I both know He can even use undergarments.

Job was one of those exceptions to the "disobedience brings judgment" rule that I mentioned earlier. He was a righteous, upright, godly man — but God allowed Satan to wreak havoc on Job's life in order to prove Job's faithfulness to God. Job didn't claim to be perfect, but he knew he hadn't committed any sin so serious that it warranted the loss of everything he held dear. I can relate so well to Job since my reaction to God after 9/11 was very similar. Job and I both challenged God and demanded answers from Him, asking, "Why, why, why is this happening to me?" In Job 28:12, Job says, "But where can wisdom be found? Where is the place of understanding?" Eight verses later, Job repeats himself. "Where can wisdom be found? Where is the place of understanding?" Eight verses later, Job answers himself. "Behold, the fear of the LORD (*yi'rah*), that is wisdom. And to depart from evil, that is understanding." Like Job, I finally got it. The treasure of wisdom can only be found in trusting and obeying the Lord and His Word.

I'm pleased to announce that once the radiation treatments were over, I was granted permission to wear the undergarment of my choice. I can also go to the beach and wear deodorant, and I no longer have to secure anything when I run down a flight of stairs. And if nothing else came from the underwire experience, at least I have a better handle on fearing the LORD. *Yi'rah.*

Guard, through the Holy Spirit who dwells in us,
the treasure which has been entrusted to you.

~2 *Timothy 1:14*

Classified Gems

3

If we own an object of great value, we usually take good care of it. Or at least, that's how it's supposed to work. Whether it's a car, a boat, a house, expensive jewelry, stocks and bonds, or an elaborate computer system, we maintain it, protect it, and may even insure it because it has great value to us. And if the object happens to be something we made, built or created *ourselves* — like an oil painting or a crocheted blanket or hand-made furniture — we usually take even better care of it because its very existence is a result of our own time, effort, and love.

But as careful as we are in caring for and protecting our treasures, it doesn't even come close to how God handles us, His most valuable treasures. God owns us. We're His property. As believers, we are not our own. We were bought at a price (1 COR. 6:19-20). We're God's treasured possessions, and He protects us the way a Father protects His children: "See how great a love the Father has bestowed on us, that we would be called children of God; and such we are" (1 JOHN 3:1). He also protects His treasures the way a shepherd protects his sheep. Jesus said, "I am the good shepherd; the good shepherd lays down His life for the sheep" (JOHN 10:11). Even before Jesus made His grand entrance on earth, the prophet Isaiah wrote about God's protection and ownership of us: "Fear not, for I have redeemed you; I have called you by your name; you are Mine" (ISA.43:1, NKJV).

My friend Jim Herndon, who is a missionary for Word of Life, once shared his thoughts on "treasure" with me. He said everything that we believe to be valuable fits into at least one of these categories: it is either unique, versatile, durable, or it has sentimental value. Some treasures meet all four criteria. Some only meet one or two. And there may be more criteria that we haven't thought of yet — feel free to e-mail me if you come up with any.

Think of someone or something that has tremendous worth to you. Right now I'm thinking of my family and my home. But on close inspection of my value system, I must ask myself: Is God as much a treasure to me as I am to Him? Do I treat Him with as much love and respect and protection as I do my most valuable possessions? Do I classify and guard Him as my most precious gem? Or do I stick Him in the same box as my costume jewelry? I have been guilty of all of the above. Chances are, so have you.

Yet in spite of our folly, our fraudulence, our frailty, our faithlessness, and our failures, God thinks we're pretty special. In His eyes, we meet all four of those criteria: we're unique, we're versatile, we're durable, and we have sentimental value. We meet all His standards for being classified as a treasure, and as such, He handles us with the utmost care.

Read the next four chapters and you'll see what I mean.

·ʧ·

*For we are His workmanship, created in Christ Jesus for good works,
which God prepared beforehand so that we would walk in them.*

~Ephesians 2:10

One of a Kind

4

As a pharmacist, I enjoy collecting antique pharmacy memorabilia — pills and potions from long-ago generations, before the modern days of corporate pharmaceutical manufacturers. I once paid an antique dealer fifty dollars for a two-ounce bottle of Pinex cough syrup. Why? Because the bottle of potent elixir dated back to the 1930s and according to the label, its main ingredient was *chloroform*. Oh yeah, I'm sure patients stopped coughing after taking it — and they probably stopped breathing, too. Back in the 1800s, chloroform was used for general anesthesia, but it soon proved to be extremely toxic and even deadly for human exposure or consumption. It has long since been banned from consumer products and its existence is scarce, which is why that old bottle of Pinex has such great value. Not that I will ever use it, mind you. I keep it on display in a locked cabinet along with other unique apothecary treasures like Worm Lozenges and Strychnine tablets. They make great conversation pieces.

According to Wikipedia, da Vinci's painting of Mona Lisa is currently valued at $670 million dollars. One oil portrait of one unattractive lady painted by one Italian artist who would never have been able to conceive of that much money in his time. Yes, beauty is in the eye of the beholder, but one cannot argue with a price tag. The more uncommon or unusual an object it is, the more value it has — whether it's an old bottle of cough syrup or an original oil painting.

Each one of us is a unique treasure to God. He designed each of us in His own likeness; yet we are completely unique and individual, which makes us extremely valuable. We are, as Psalm 139 proclaims, "fearfully and wonderfully made" — exclusive and distinctive masterpieces of His brilliance. Even identical twins are not completely identical; there are no two sets of fingerprints alike in this world. When God was at the drawing board, He said, "Let Us make man in Our image, according to Our likeness" (GEN. 1:26). So we were intended to be reflections of God's glory in His very character, nature, and perfection. Even when our parents crashed in the Garden and the curse of sin entered our hearts, God still treasured us. I think about all the times I have disobeyed Him and disrespected Him, all the times when I did *not* treasure Him, and I am amazed at the way Jesus made it possible for me to be forgiven. He was willing to go on a deadly mission to pay the full price for me. That clearly demonstrates that I am a unique treasure to Him.

And He is a unique treasure to us. The nature of our Triune God is a mystery — it's impossible for our limited human minds to explain or even understand how one eternal being exists and manifests Himself in three distinct persons. God the Father is the one, true, living God — El Shaddai, God Almighty — and there is nothing or no one else like Him. Jesus is unique because He is fully God, possessing all divine power and authority; yet He is fully man, and the only perfect and sinless human being to have walked this earth. And the Holy Spirit is like no other. Since He is the divine power by which we come to Jesus and see with new eyes of faith, He is closer to us than we are to ourselves.

Since we were created in His likeness, God's unique status demands something unique from us. God says, "Therefore be holy, for I am holy" (LEV. 11:44). Paul says, "Do not be con-

18

formed to this world, but be transformed by the renewing of your mind" (ROM. 12:2). In other words, don't be like the commoner — be like the King. As God's children, we are instructed to be set apart and distinct from the world. We should *seek to be unique*. (Someone should put that on a T-shirt.)

So God is unique treasure indeed — no question there. He is also my only source of true happiness, and therefore my only source for true riches. Other people or things may satisfy me temporarily, but God fills much deeper needs. Only Jesus could pay the high price for my salvation, and only Jesus could love me enough to actually go through with it. Only Jesus said, "I am the way, and the truth, and the life; no one comes to the Father but through Me" (JOHN 14:6). He didn't say He was one of several ways or truths. He said He is *the* way and *the* truth and *the* life — as in *the one and only*, solitary, exclusive, unique way, truth, and life. He alone gives me joy and peace and wisdom and comfort. He alone promises me eternal life. He alone is unique treasure, and I bow down to Him alone.

How blessed is the man who finds wisdom and the man who gains understanding. For her profit is better than the profit of silver and her gain better than fine gold. She is more precious than jewels; and nothing you desire compares with her.

~Proverbs 3:13-17

Multi-faceted

5

In the movie *My Big Fat Greek Wedding*, the bride's father used Windex® for its versatility in treating everything from fabric stains to acne. Personally, I think that movie is one of the most hilarious films ever made — probably because I relate to it so well. Even though we're not Greek, that movie could easily have been about me and my Italian family. We're not nearly as big or as loud as they were, but we do have some similar habits. Instead of using Windex for every purpose under the sun, we use olive oil. We cook with it. We dip our bread in it (instead of using butter). We clean with it. We polish our furniture with it. We use it as a moisturizer for our skin and a cuticle remover for our nails. During my radiation treatments, I was prescribed a special topical cream for radiation burns. Its main ingredient? Yup, olive oil. In Jenniferland, olive oil is indispensable. It is versatile treasure.

Versatile treasure is multifaceted, flexible, adaptable to different situations, and used for many different purposes. My dad carries a small Leatherman tool in his pocket every day. I can't tell you how many times that thing has come in handy when we needed a box opened or a screw tightened. But olive oil and a Leatherman tool pale in comparison to the most common versatile treasure: money. There are few things in this world that we can't obtain with cold hard cash. And since we live in a plastic, automated generation of credit cards and calling cards and gift cards and bank cards, money is becoming even more flexible. Versatile treasures have such great value that you don't leave home without them — lest you'll regret it.

But the Beatles were occasionally right: money can't buy me love. And the Bible is always right: money can't buy our salvation. There will be no use for money, pocket knives, Windex®, or olive oil in heaven, so I best not get too attached to them. The book of Ecclesiastes rightly proclaims the futility of pleasure and possessions. Solomon found out the hard way: "I collected for myself silver and gold and the treasure of kings and provinces... behold all was vanity and striving after the wind and there was no profit under the sun" (ECCL. 2:8).

Poor Solomon. He started out so great, so focused on the Lord. But his possessions and his women redirected his vision away from God. I can see how easily that could happen, and I thank God for using Solomon to warn me of the danger. He taught me that instead of *possessing* versatile treasures for myself, I should strive to *be* a versatile treasure for God, who gives us many different purposes and ways to serve Him. Each of us is given at least one spiritual gift (making us unique treasures indeed) along with opportunities to use that gift for God's glory. Paul told the Corinthian believers, "There are varieties of gifts, but the same Spirit. There are varieties of ministries, and the same Lord. There are varieties of effects, but the same God who works all things in all persons" (1 COR. 12:4-6). Loosely paraphrased: we are versatile treasures with various purposes serving the same God.

22   Before September 11, I used to think that my primary purpose in life was to be a good wife to my husband and to dispense prescription medications to our community. Sure, I had other responsibilities and dreams, but I definitely had no aspiration to serve the Lord. Not that being a happily married pharmacist

wasn't an honorable position to hold, but God knew that my usefulness in His kingdom was limited. Back then, I was a treasure to Him — but not necessarily a versatile one. He needed to make me versatile.

I can still clearly recall that day in third grade (circa 1973) when I had strep throat and had to stay home from school. My teacher, Mrs. Baker, had given us a writing assignment that was due in a few days. As I sat in bed sick, I worked on the essay so I wouldn't be too far behind with homework.

My mother came into my bedroom with a bowl of chicken soup. As she set up the tray table next to the bed, I clearly remember saying these words: "Mom, guess what? I know what I wanna be when I grow up!"

She said, "Really? What?"

I proudly exclaimed, "An author!"

And she said, "That's nice, dear. Now eat your soup." Then she left the room.

That was the last time I ever thought about writing as a career. That is, until God opened the door thirty years later. And after I walked through the Author door, He opened the Speaker door. So now when people ask what I do for a living, I say, "It depends on what day of the week it is. I juggle three different jobs. I'm a Christian writer, a Christian speaker, and a legal drug dealer." That answer often sparks their curiosity and opens the Testimony door.

By the way, Mom has no recollection of that conversation about my future endeavor. But in her defense, she is the strongest supporter of my ministry and she still makes me chicken soup when I'm sick.

It's only by the manifold grace (the versatile treasure) of God that I have been given the gifts of writing and speaking, and the opportunities to serve the Lord with them. Peter explains it this way: "As each one has received a special gift, employ it in serving one another as good stewards of the manifold grace of God. Whoever speaks is to do so as one who is speaking the utterances of God; whoever serves is to do so as one who is serving by the strength which God supplies; so that in all things God may be glorified through Jesus Christ, to whom belongs the glory and dominion forever and ever. Amen" (1 PET. 4:10-11). I say, amen again. If I am indeed now a versatile treasure in God's eyes, it is only because He has made me that way. *Thank You, Lord, thank You.* To borrow the words of the Psalmist: "Not unto me, Lord, not unto me, but to Your name I give glory; because of Your mercy, because of Your truth" (PS. 115:1, NKJV). If we allow God to equip us and work in our life, we can become versatile treasure to Him.

It's hard to imagine that we could be anything worthwhile to the Creator of the universe. But it's easy to see how He is a versatile treasure to us. After all, in Exodus 3:14 He says, "I AM WHO I AM" and that pretty much covers it all. The Lord plays so many different roles in our lives that I often ask myself how I ever lived without Him all those years! The answer? By His grace. He carried me in His arms even before I acknowledged Him as my Lord and Savior. In Ephesians 3:10 Paul declares "the manifold wisdom of God," and, as I mentioned earlier, Peter declares "the manifold grace of God" (1 PET. 4:10). I love that word *manifold*. It means "variegated or multifaceted," the way that many different facets of a diamond reflect and enhance its beauty.

God is manifold, versatile treasure and the Bible is His resume. Samuel gives us just a small portion of it: "The LORD is my rock and my fortress and my deliverer... my shield, and the horn of my salvation, my stronghold and my refuge; my savior" (2 SAM. 22:2-3). David adds to it: He is "a father to the fatherless and a defender of widows" (PS. 68:5, NIV). As I read those words — rock, shield, stronghold, refuge, deliverer, father, defender of widows — I find myself tearing up and nodding in agreement. *Yes, yes, yes, Lord, You have shown me that You are all of those and more.*

I think of Jesus saying, "*I am* the bread of life" (JOHN 6:35), and I know that, like food, I cannot sustain my life without Him. When He says, "*I am* the light of the world" (JOHN 8:12), I realize that without Him I lived in darkness — even though I didn't realize how dark it really was until He turned the light on. When He says, "*I am* the good shepherd" (JOHN 10:11), I clearly see that truth in my life — His guidance, His protection, His tender care and love. And the versatility of His job description goes on and on. "*I am* the resurrection and the life" (JOHN 11:25). "*I am* the true vine" (JOHN 15:1). "*I am* the way, the truth, and the life" (JOHN 14:6). Jesus even said, "When you lift up the Son of Man, then you will know that I AM He" (JOHN 8:28, NKJV), and "Most assuredly I say to you, before Abraham was, I AM" (JOHN 8:58, NKJV). In making those bold statements, Jesus used the Hebrew name for LORD (which is YHWH or Yahweh, meaning "I AM") and in doing so, He claimed to be God and risked being stoned for blasphemy. But this wasn't just some delusional person claiming to be God. He really *was* God. He really *is* God. In Revelation chapter 1 He says, "I AM the Alpha and the Omega... I AM the first and the last." When Jesus says "*I am*," He means He *really is*.

He is enough. He is more than enough. He is everything. He is versatile treasure. He is God.

The grass withers, the flower fades,
but the word of our God stands forever.

~Isaiah 40:8

A Diamond
Is Forever

6

A few years ago, I had the old gray carpet in the living/dining area of my house ripped up and hardwood floors put down. (No, I did not do this work myself — I'm not that versatile.) Before the new wooden planks were installed, I invited my family and church friends to come over and write their favorite Bible verse on the sub-flooring with a thick, black, permanent marker. The floor was covered with Scripture from one end of the room to another, along with their names and the date they wrote their verse. Some of them got creative. In the area where the piano would be placed, my brother, Anthony, wrote Ephesians 5:19-20: "Sing and make music in your heart to the Lord, always giving thanks to God for everything in the name of our Lord Jesus Christ." Under the dining room table, my brother-in-law, Tom, wrote John 6:35: "Jesus said to them, 'I am the bread of life. He who comes to me will not hunger and he who believes in me will never thirst.'" My own contribution was Jeremiah 29:11, my life verse: "For I know the plans I have for you," says the Lord. "Plans for good and not for evil; to give you hope and a future." The hardwood floors were eventually laid on top of our Bible verses and now, as we walk around that room, we can say that we're "standing on the promises of God."

Hardwood floors are strong, sturdy, and resilient; and they

don't wear out quickly. In the material world, we usually pay more for such durable items because they last longer and are therefore more valuable. Leather shoes last longer than inexpensive, man-made imitations. A hard-cover book will sustain wear much longer than a paperback. I am willing to pay more for a reputable brand of house paint because the cheaper store brands often chip and peel or require too many coats. With respect to durability, you usually get what you pay for.

In life, we become more durable when we persevere and endure through our trials. In my high school gym class, we were required to run track. I was great at sprinting, but I was not a good endurance runner. I was pretty much down for the count after just one mile. (And things haven't changed since then.) In the marathon of life, it's my endurance — not my speed — that will win the race. James says, "Blessed is the man who perseveres under trial, because when he has stood the test, he will receive the crown of life that God has promised to those who love Him" (JAMES 1:12, NIV).

I'm not very useful to the Lord if I tire out quickly and throw in the towel early. Believe me, there were several times throughout the writing of this book when I was close to shutting down the whole operation. Days during the radiation treatments when I was exhausted and in pain... days when the thoughts weren't coming as quickly as the deadlines... days when my computer was misbehaving... days when everything that could go wrong did go wrong. But God gave me all the grace I needed to persevere through those struggles. Like hardwood floors, my value is partially determined by how well I hold up when people or things walk all over me. The more durable I am, the more valuable I am to God; and fortunately, He gives me the strength I need to become durable.

Isaiah says, "Those who wait for the LORD will gain new strength; they will mount up with wings like eagles, they will run and not get tired, they will walk and not become weary" (ISA. 40:31). That cute pink rabbit keeps going and going, but eventually he gets tired and weary and he kicks the bucket. With God as my power source, I can do all things through Him who strengthens me. The writer of Hebrews tells us to "run with endurance the race that is set before us, fixing our eyes on Jesus, the author and perfecter of faith" (HEB. 12:1-2). Jesus paid so much for me — I want to give Him a good return on His investment. I want to be a durable treasure for Him, just as He is for me.

It always reassures me to know that God has always existed and will always exist. Hebrews 13 reminds me that God is durable treasure — He is the same yesterday, today, and forever — eternal, permanent, and unchanging. Jesus Himself defines endurance. Throughout His life on earth, He endured so much criticism and rejection and betrayal. He endured temptations and accusations and confrontations and condemnations. And at the end of His thirty-three-year marathon, He endured unspeakable agony on the cross as He suffered for mankind. When I read through the Gospels, I marvel at Jesus' steadfastness — His unwavering stability and His unrelenting love for us. They are the durable treasures that brought Him to victory.

Let's go back to my hardwood floor. The beautiful, natural grain of the wood is lovely and I expect to be walking on it for decades. I'm sure it will increase the selling price of my home, but the real value is what lies hidden underneath the floorboards. My hope is that after I'm long gone, someone will pull up those old floors and discover the treasure underneath. It'll be like an archaeological dig. Maybe they will be believers and the Scripture verses will be a huge encouragement for their faith. Maybe they won't be believers and the verses will give them every reason to become one, like when they read Hebrews 10:34 near the front window: "You can have a better and enduring possession for yourselves in heaven."

The Bible is many things, including durable. It has been divinely preserved for thousands of years, and it promises to remain that way. Jesus said, "Heaven and earth will pass away, but My words will not pass away" (MATT. 24:35). With durable treasures, we usually get what we pay for. Yet amazingly, we can get eternal life even though we didn't pay for it. By God's grace through faith in His Son, *we* get what *Jesus* paid for, and that will last forever.

·ƒ·

"They shall be Mine," says the LORD of hosts,
"on the day that I make them My jewels."

~Malachi 3:17

Keepsakes

7

On the landing of the staircase in my house sits a tall, slender ceramic planter with a pretty floral and leaf design on it. I never put a plant in it — I kill plants. Its purpose is for display, not function. I bought it on sale for fifteen bucks at Pier 1 Imports many years ago. One day, Jim was coming down the stairs carrying a big box. He miscalculated his clearance and the box hit the planter and the planter hit the floor, breaking into a hundred pieces. I really was not upset about this. After all, it was just a cheap, decorative, oversized knick-knack. But Jim felt awful about breaking it.

"I'll buy you a new one, hon," he said, trying desperately to redeem himself, even though he knew he'd never find another one exactly like it. I have no doubt that he would have replaced it with a Waterford Crystal planter if I had shed even one single tear over the incident. I reassured him that it really wasn't a big deal, and to please not fret about it.

About a week later, I came home from work and headed upstairs. There on the landing stood my planter — once again intact. Jim had painstakingly glued all the tiny, jagged-edged, broken pieces together — a project that had clearly taken much time, patience, and love. That planter still sits on the landing of my stairs. It has glue globs and jigsaw-puzzle lines and a curiously odd shape, but it is worth far more to me now than it ever

33

could have before it crashed. It is a treasure with great sentimental value.

It's sentimental value that gives objects a special place in our hearts. Attics are filled with them. The birthday card that your eight-year old made for you. A lock of hair from your first haircut. Photographs of you and your best friend at high school graduation. They may be worthless to everyone else, but they have such cherished meaning to us that we can't put a price on them.

We have that kind of sentimental value to God, and this amazes me. So often I have stumbled through life apathetic to His love, and yet I (we) hold such a special place in the heart of Christ that He left His throne in heaven to save us from being permanently separated from Him. For those of us who put our trust in Him, He takes all the broken pieces of our lives and glues them together with His grace and love, forming a permanent bond. Even if other people might not think so much of us, God went to the greatest extreme to show all of us His love. We have unsurpassed sentimental value to Him.

Because of that love, we should value God in that same way. Every time I climb my staircase, I look at the broken vase that Jim repaired and I think of his heart full of love. But sometimes (not often enough) I stop and look at it through different eyes. I think of how broken my life was after 9/11, and how Jesus put me back together again and made me a new creation. I think of His heart full of love and I just want to cry. Sentimental treasure will do that. It's a tearjerker.

If I tried to sell that broken vase at a yard sale (which of course I'd never do), I'd probably have to pay someone to take it off my hands. One man's treasure is another man's junk, and vice versa. Sadly, we don't all put the same value on what Jesus accomplished on the cross. Paul told the Corinthians, "For indeed Jews ask for signs and Greeks search for wisdom; but we preach

34

Christ crucified, to Jews a stumbling block and to Gentiles foolishness, but to those who are the called, both Jews and Greeks, Christ the power of God and the wisdom of God" (1 COR. 1:22-24). If life were a yard sale, many people would walk right on by and disregard the sentimental treasure of Jesus. They might even mock and ridicule us for placing such value on Him. The treasure of salvation is free for the asking, yet sometimes God can't even give it away.

As for me, I thank God for bringing blessings out of my brokenness. I was broken from sin, I was broken from grief, I was broken from cancer, I was broken from weariness. I cannot put a price on Him "Who pardons all your iniquities, Who heals all your diseases, Who redeems your life from the pit, Who crowns you with lovingkindness and compassion; Who satisfies your years with good things, so that your youth is renewed like the eagle" (PS. 103:3-5). He is unique, He is versatile, He is durable, and He has unlimited sentimental value. He is my greatest treasure.

A cross made of two beams of olive wood? $100. Three long nails and a hammer? $15. An innocent carpenter willing to take the death penalty for our sins? Priceless.

Thus says the LORD, "Let not a wise man boast of his wisdom, and let not the mighty man boast of his might, let not a rich man boast of his riches; but let him who boasts boast of this: that he understands and knows Me, that I am the LORD who exercises lovingkindness, justice, and righteousness on earth; for I delight in these things," declares the LORD."

~Jeremiah 9:23-24

More Precious
than Silver

8

Out of the origi-
nal five members of our family unit — my parents, my sister, my
brother, and me — three of us have been treated for cancer. That's
60 percent of our family — a shocking statistic. I battled breast
cancer and survived. My dad battled prostate cancer and survived.
My brother, Anthony, was diagnosed with a terminal brain tumor
in July 2000. He was not expected to live six months; but after
several surgeries and many rounds of chemotherapy and radiation treatments, the cancer went into remission.

We realize that God could have chosen *not* to heal us; He
certainly has divine authority to veto our desperate appeals. We
also realize that cancer can appear or recur in any of us, at any
time in the future. If that should happen, we are committed to
once again trusting God and His plan for us.

In fact, we recently found ourselves back in that familiar territory. In the summer of 2008, Anthony's brain tumor returned with a
vengeance. His doctors said, "No more surgery or radiation. He's
had too much of both. Chemotherapy is the only option." Well,
chemo might be the only option doctors offer, and we'll take it...
but prayer has its own power, and I've been on my knees ever since.

*Lord, I realize that I'm being selfish and greedy by
asking You for more time with Anthony... after all,*

*the doctors gave him six months and You've gra-
ciously given him eight years. But I also can't hide
what's in my heart: I want more time. We want
more time. Please give the doctors wisdom and
skill beyond all human capability. Nevertheless, let
not my will, but Yours, be done. Please give all of
us the strength to accept whatever You choose for
Anthony's life.*

The apostle Paul
was well-acquainted with desperate prayers for healing. Paul told
the Corinthian believers about his affliction with a "thorn in the
flesh." We don't know what his physical condition was, but we
know it caused him a lot of grief. Paul said, "Concerning this I
implored the Lord three times that it might leave me" (2 COR.
12:8). We've all been there before. I know I have. Pleading with
God to relieve my pain. Begging Him to restore my life. Implor-
ing Him to take the cup away. Perhaps you're there right now,
and you wonder why the Lord is allowing you or your loved one
to suffer with no end in sight.

In spite of Paul's appeal, God did not remove the thorn, and
His answer to Paul was, "My grace is sufficient for you, for power
is perfected in weakness" (2 COR. 12:9). Instead of resolving
Paul's pain, God promised to reveal His divine power through
Paul, and that He did. Since Paul was forced to completely rely
upon the Lord for his strength, his ministry became even more
successful. That was a far better solution than removing the
thorn, and only God could have known it. Paul goes on to say,
"Most gladly, therefore, I will rather boast about my weaknesses,
so that the power of Christ may dwell in me. Therefore I am
well content with weaknesses, with insults, with distresses, with
persecutions, with difficulties, for Christ's sake; for when I am
weak, then I am strong" (2 COR. 12:9-10). You might be praying

38

right now for God to take away your thorn in the flesh. There's nothing wrong with that. But God doesn't always give us everything we want; instead, He gives us everything we need.

Scripture gives us some answers on the subject of "Why Does God Allow Suffering?"; and I love how the Lord provides us with those little treasures of comfort in His Word. After all, He is under no obligation to rationalize or validate His motives to us, and we should never feel rightfully entitled to any explanations. But God knows our human desire to satisfy our curiosity in order to endure our trials; so with His never-ending grace, He'll sometimes let us glimpse a corner of the blueprint so we can say, "Aahh, *now* I see where You're going with this."

But if God continually exposed corners of His providential plan, we'd never learn to build confidence in His power and sovereignty. I like what Christian apologist Ravi Zacharias once said on his radio program: "On the basis of what I do know about God, I can trust Him with the things that I don't know." The problem for many people is that they just don't know God. They might *think* they know Him. They know *of* Him. They know *about* Him. But they don't personally and intimately *know* Him.

In the English language, when we say we "know" someone or something, it generally means that we are acquainted with that person or we have information or facts about that thing — the way we "know" the cashier at the supermarket or the way we "know" how to make a killer lasagna (and I do). But in Hebrew, the verb "to know" (*yada*, accent on the second syllable) takes on a far broader meaning, especially when it's in reference to the knowledge of God (*da'at Elohim*). The Jewish concept of the "knowledge" of a person (or God) refers to a close, personal relationship or experience with that person (or with God), the way a child knows their parent or a husband knows his wife. Unlike the word *knowledge* in the English language, the Hebrew *yada* does not mean an academic understanding or an accumulation of facts. It's not only about knowing who someone is, it's also about having a fondness and affection for them. I had a much different knowledge of my husband than did the guy who always filled up Jim's fuel tank at the gas station. (In case you're wondering, self-serve pumps are illegal in New Jersey so we can't pump our own gas. I don't even know how to pump my own gas.) We might *think* we know the neighbor down the street because we wave to them on the way to work each morning. We might *think* we know Oprah Winfrey because we watch her on television or read about her in magazines. We might "know" them, but we do not *yada* them.

The only way you really get to *yada* someone is to spend quality time with them on a regular basis. That's when you discover who they really are and what they're really like. You get to know their character, their nature, their heart. You get to know how trustworthy they really are (or how trustworthy they're not). And it's the same way with God. The only way we really get to know God — *da'at Elohim* — is to spend quality time with Him on a regular basis.

In my B.C. days, I had a much different definition of "quality time" and "regular basis" than I do now. I used to think that spending quality time with the Lord on a regular basis meant spending one hour in church, once a week. After all, that was sufficient for the relationship I had with my hairdresser or some of my co-workers. But spending only one hour a week with Jim would have been unthinkable. How much more, then, should I want to spend time with my Father in heaven, my Creator, my Savior?

Thanks to Jerry Seinfeld, the expression "*yada yada yada*" has become a standard part of the English vocabulary, virtually replacing "et cetera" and providing a convenient, new sound bite for "you-know-what-I'm-talking-about-so-I'm-not-going-to-waste-time-explaining-it." In the Hebrew language, anything re-peated three times is done so for strong emphasis on the point being made. Since Jerry Seinfeld is Jewish, I don't think he'd mind if I take his sitcom's popular line, translate it into Hebrew, and apply it to my life mission: *Yada Yada Yada.* Get to know God personally... Get to know God personally... Get to know God personally...

Therefore everyone who hears these words of Mine and acts on them,
may be compared to a wise man who built his house on the rock.
And the rain fell, and the floods came, and the winds blew
and slammed against that house;
and yet it did not fall,
for it had been founded on the rock.

~Matthew 7:24-25

Rock of Ages

9

For thirty-eight years of my life, I never opened a Bible nor did I have any interest in doing so. Before September 11, I had no heart for Jesus. No heart for Scripture. No heart for things eternal. I was living quite comfortably and I saw no necessity for what I called "religious stuff." But the "food" and the "light" in my life were coming from sources that would not have sustained my spiritual health for a lifetime (this one or the next). Yes, I was blessed with a loving husband and a wonderful marriage. But the material treasures I once thought were so valuable turned out to be worthless in the scope of eternity. Cars and boats and jewelry and big-screen TVs didn't give me nearly as much satisfaction as I now receive from reading the Bible, hearing a good sermon, or talking with Yeshua every day. Scripture showed me how needy I really was — it showed me the treasure that was missing in my life — and then it pointed me to the Savior. That's where the real "food" and "light" comes from, and God gently reminds me of those priorities on a regular basis.

Let me illustrate. Recently, my family and I vacationed in Bermuda, that beautiful little island in the Atlantic Ocean off the coast of North Carolina. Unlike most islands in the nearby Caribbean, Bermuda's waters can have strong currents and surges.

My sister Maria and I had brought our inflatable rafts so we could float in those turquoise waters and soak up the sun. But there were many large rocks jutting out of the water, dotting the landscape of the ocean, so we had to be careful not to float into them. With the strong current in the water, we had to continually paddle ourselves to stay close to the beach and to avoid the rocks. This quickly became a tiring chore and we tried to think of a way to attach our rafts to the rocks so we wouldn't drift away. We agreed that a rope would be ideal, but there was none to be found.

Until the next morning. Behold, a small boat that had been shipwrecked somewhere washed up overnight on the shores of our hotel's beach. (What are the chances of that?) And attached to the boat, as a sweet little gift from God, was — you guessed it — a rope. "Delight yourself in the Lord and He will give you the desires of your heart" (PS. 37:4). Thank You, Lord, for putting that desire on our hearts, and thank You for actually providing it! God doesn't miss a beat. He pays attention to every little detail in our lives. If it matters to us, then it matters to Him.

I untied the rope from the remains of the boat and took our rafts out into the water. I found a large rock shaped like an anvil and secured one end of the rope to it. That left several feet of rope for us to hold onto while keeping us far enough away from the rock. So we climbed onto our rafts, and I held on to the loose end of the rope while Maria held on to my raft. We closed our eyes and let the sun beat down on us while the sound of gentle waves broke on the shore. We were anchored to the rock, and it was sheer bliss.

We enjoyed it so much that we tried it again the next day. This time, however, the tide had come in. The water was deeper and the current was even stronger. The high tide had completely submerged our rock, but that wasn't going to stop me. I simply found a different rock. I made a double knot around it and we once again resumed positions, only this time we reversed our roles — Maria was the official rope-holder while I held onto her raft. We closed our eyes and let the sun beat down on us while the sound of gentle waves broke on the shore. We were anchored to the rock and it was sheer bliss.

About twenty minutes later, Maria let out a loud gasp. Her outburst shattered the peace of our floating paradise and probably startled every fish in the vicinity. I sat up and looked over at her: dazed and confused, Maria was holding both ends of the rope.

The rope had become untied from the surge of the current, and we had been cluelessly floating on our cute pink rafts with a firm grip on a very useless rope dragging along behind us. We had drifted so far that we were already in the vicinity of the next hotel's beach — a football field away. Since the shore was made of rocks instead of sand, we were forced to swim. It took a whole lotta paddlin' against a strong current to get ourselves back to where we started. Lesson learned. Like the old hymn goes, "Be very sure, be very sure, your anchor holds and grips the Solid Rock."[1]

Sometimes I think I'm anchored to the Rock of Christ, but the high tides and currents of life can jeopardize my grip on Him and the pleasantries (or the unpleasantries) of life distract me. My anchor line begins to loosen, but I'm too busy to notice. Before long, I've drifted into unknown or even dangerous territory.

The writer of Hebrews says, "This hope we have as an anchor of the soul, a hope both sure and steadfast..." (6:19). The word *hope* in that passage (and many times in the New Testament) does not mean "wishful thinking" or optimistic expectations, as it does in our English language — the way we hope that dress goes on sale or hope it doesn't rain tomorrow. Instead, it means absolute certainty. Divine assurance. The hope — our anchor, our rock — is Jesus Christ and His Word. He is secure and immovable. The anchor doesn't move, I do. *I* move when I allow myself

45

to become disconnected. It takes regular check-ups to make sure that my anchor line stays moored to Christ so I don't drift away from Him.

Staying connected to God is what gives me clarity of His purpose and constant reminders of His character. That connection comes through consistent prayer and fellowship with Him. Through consistent Bible reading and study. By consistently examining my anchor lines and addressing any issues or sins in my life that could loosen the knot. It's all about consistency. There are days when I spend many hours talking to Yeshua and reading His Word, and I so thoroughly enjoy it that I have to force myself to stop for lunch or to go to work. But other days, it's not so easy. I seem to find every excuse to put off my devotional time with the Lord. I forget what a gift — what a treasure — my prayer time is. Through Jesus, I have direct access to the Creator of the universe, who actually makes time for me — a staggering concept in itself. Yet I sometimes reschedule our appointment because... well... other things seem more important at the moment.

Inside my prayer journal, there is a quote from the nineteenth-century South African pastor Andrew Murray. It says: "How does Satan hinder prayer? By temptation to postpone or curtail it, by bringing in wandering thoughts and all sorts of distractions, through unbelief and hopelessness."[2]

Wandering thoughts indeed. I wish I had a spam-filter for my brain. I don't know what "spam" stands for in the computer industry (does it stand for anything?); but in the spiritual world, I think spam should stand for Satan's Plot Against Mankind. So the wandering thoughts and the temptations to postpone prayer do come. But what jolts me back into action is the idea that since Satan is tempting me to delay or dismiss my devotional time, he must really feel threatened by something I intend to pray about. *Well do me a favor, Lucifer. You got a problem? Take it up with my Father.*

If I relax my priorities, then I'm headed for trouble. If I slack off in my daily prayers and Bible reading, I'll eventually find myself in unfamiliar (or even dangerous) territory. Remember, if Maria and I had consistently examined the rope to make sure it was still secure, then our legs and biceps wouldn't have been so sore the next day. But thanks be to God for the Rock of Christ — at least He doesn't move! Because His Word is absolute truth, I am secure in His promises. The tides and currents of life will change, but Jesus Christ is durable treasure — He's the same yesterday, today, and forever. Like an anchor holding a ship safely in position, I am moored to the Lord.

Hey, there's another good idea for a T-shirt.

...the kingdom of heaven is like a merchant seeking fine pearls,
and upon finding one pearl of great value, he went and
sold all that he had and bought it.

~Matthew 13:45-46

Where the
Heart Is

10

I'm really not big
into jewelry. I have no good explanation for that. I have a handful of very special pieces (which Jim bought me) that I wear on
special occasions. I still wear my engagement and wedding rings
every day, but otherwise I'm minimally adorned by choice.

The fact that I still wear my engagement and wedding rings
has proven to be confusing for some people. Either they assume
I've remarried, or they find it very odd that I would continue to
wear them as a widow. When they ask me about it, I tell them
that the rings still symbolize the love that Jim and I had for each
other, but now they have an additional meaning: they represent
the commitment I have made to Jesus, and the unending love
He has for me. Some people are satisfied with that answer. Some
people get teary-eyed and say, "Oh, that's sooo beautiful..." Others just walk away perplexed, scratching their heads.

Another piece of jewelry that I wear every day is my cross
necklace, and that has a story of its own. If you've read *A Tempered Faith*, you may recall the chapter titled "The Rose and the
Lenox Vase," in which I described myself as a single, red rose and
Jim as an expensive vase. A flower, by itself, is beautiful. A vase,
displayed by itself, is a work of art. Alone, Jim and I were lovely;
together, we made each other shine. But one day, the vase came

crashing to the ground and left the rose all by herself. She was alone — devastated, lost, thirsty, and dying.

As the rose, I had a choice: either shrivel up and become a stick of thorns or look for water so I would live and never thirst again. Jesus offered me living water (JOHN 4:14). I immersed myself and found new life in Him.

After my best friend Amy read the manuscript for *Tempered*, she was deeply touched by that chapter and gave me a gift — a unique and sentimental treasure — the most beautiful silver cross necklace I've ever seen. This simple description will do it no justice: there is a silver rosebud in the center of the cross and its stems and leaves extend out to form the beams. And Amy's words to me were the best part of the gift: "Now the rose isn't dying by itself anymore. Now the rose is alive, *with* the cross."

She summed up my whole testimony with one profound statement. And since the same people who ask about my wedding ring usually ask about my necklace, too, I get to share this story with them. The cross necklace is not just material treasure made of sterling silver, it's also spiritual treasure because it's a great witnessing tool for the love of Christ. Jesus, who wore a crown of thorns for me, went to Calvary so that I could one day be an eternal rose with Him. "In Him we have redemption through His blood, the forgiveness of our trespasses, according to the riches of His grace which He lavished on us" (EPH. 1:7). *That* is a treasure. That is treasured faith.

As long as we're on the subject of jewelry...

The last birthday present that Jim bought for me — in April of 2001 — was a pair of genuine pearl and diamond earrings. They are beautifully simple and elegant. He picked them out all by himself and I couldn't have picked anything nicer if I had my choice.

I never fully understood how a pearl is formed until recently. It's produced within the soft tissue of a living, shelled mollusk (usually an oyster). When a parasite or a grain of sand irritates the mollusk, it reacts by secreting a substance inside its shell, which seals off the irritation. (Don't you wish you could do that to mosquitoes and telephone solicitors?) The substance is calcium carbonate, and it is deposited in concentric layers or growth rings — that's what gives the pearl its round shape. Almost any oyster can produce some kind of "pearl," but most of them have no luster, no iridescence, and no durability. Most of them aren't even attractive to look at — just a hard, ugly, glob of calcium. I wouldn't want to see *that* hanging from my ears.

The majority of the pearl industry is made up of "cultured" pearls; they're formed on a pearl farm where companies actually harvest them. But a true, "natural" pearl is one that has been formed without any human intervention at all; therefore they're unique treasure — rare and extremely valuable. So the difference between natural and cultured pearls is whether the pearl was created solely by nature (that is, God), or with the help of human hands. A natural pearl is a far greater treasure than a cultured pearl.

Pearls aren't formed easily, and they're not formed overnight. Something must irritate or disturb the oyster to begin the process, and it takes years to finish it. You probably know by now where I'm going with this. We are pearls in the hands of God, who enables our true beauty to come as a result of the trials — the irritants, the harsh conditions we experience — which form layer upon layer upon layer of spiritual maturity. The bigger a true gemstone is, the more it's worth — which puts a new perspective on the value of our suffering, right? This shows that we can have the greatest value to God and to others when we trust Him to bring forth growth from the trials we face.

These days, when I wear my pearl earrings, I think about those harsh conditions that the poor oyster endured and the stunning beauty that came from them, and I am reminded of

51

the rewards that await those of us who endure the irritants of life. I call them my James 1:12 earrings (after Jesus' brother — not my husband). "Blessed is the man who perseveres under trial; because when he has stood the test, he will receive the crown of life that God has promised to those who love him" (JAMES 1:12, NIV). The pearl earrings are another symbol of my life since 9/11 — how God has taken extreme adversity and brought blessings from it. I love how German missionary Julius Richter said it: "The burden of suffering seems to be a tombstone hung around our necks. Yet in reality, it is simply the weight necessary to hold the diver down while he is searching for pearls."3

During my cancer treatments, I rediscovered 1 Peter 1:6-7, which I had read many times before and even committed to memory. But after my diagnosis, those verses took on a whole new light. Isn't it amazing how Scripture has a way of conforming itself to whatever our current circumstances are?! Peter wrote, "In this you greatly rejoice, even though now for a little while, if necessary, you have been distressed by various trials so that the proof of your faith, being more precious than gold which is perishable, even though tested by fire, may be found to result in praise and glory and honor at the revelation of Jesus Christ." After losing Jim on September 11 and then fighting a battle with cancer (being "distressed by various trials"), my faith in God has been *tempered* and strengthened like steel or glass when it's held in a flame ("tested by fire"). My faith in God is also *teachable* as I continue to study His Word and grow in His grace ("the proof of your faith... resulting in praise, glory, and honor at the revelation of Jesus Christ"). And that same faith has become more valuable to God — *treasured* — because of those concentric layers of growth that came as a result of being tempered and teachable.

Jesus says, "Where your treasure is, there your heart will be also" (MATT. 6:21). When my jewelry box is wide open, I see my

52

wedding ring, my rosebud cross necklace, and my pearl earrings, each with their own spiritual significance. And when the treasure chest of my heart is wide open, I see the authentic precious cornerstone that shines above all else: Yeshua and His insurmountable grace and love. That's where my real treasure is, and that's where my heart is, also.

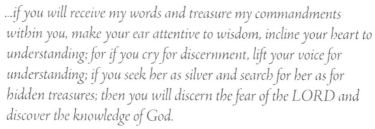

...if you will receive my words and treasure my commandments within you, make your ear attentive to wisdom, incline your heart to understanding; for if you cry for discernment, lift your voice for understanding; if you seek her as silver and search for her as for hidden treasures; then you will discern the fear of the LORD and discover the knowledge of God.

~Proverbs 2:1-5

A Certified Diamond

11

I've been a certi-
fied notary public for many years at the pharmacy where I work.
A notary helps to protect the general public against fraud by
serving as an impartial witness to the signing of important docu-
ments. But enough of the boilerplate jargon. In simple terms, my
job is to confirm that you are who you say you are (by photo
identification) and that you are the person who signed that document. You must appear before me so I can positively identify
you and physically witness your signature. Once I'm convinced
it's all legitimate, I'll sign my name, then date, stamp, and seal
the document and send you on your way.

A few years ago, a woman came into the pharmacy and needed an important legal document notarized. Her husband had
recently been killed in a motor vehicle accident, and the legal pa-
pers were necessary to process his life insurance policy. She came
to the private window in tears and my heart absolutely broke for
her. The happy life she once knew was gone, and in its place was
sorrow and turmoil. How well I could relate.

After I confirmed her identification, I watched her sign the
document. Her hands were shaking, her lips were quivering, and
a tear fell onto the page as she signed. When she put the pen
down, I took her in my arms and held her tightly as she sobbed.
I told her that I had lost my husband a few years before, and

that I understood what she was going through. Her countenance lifted when she realized she was talking to a kindred spirit, a fellow widow. We talked about the many emotions of dealing with the sudden death of a loved one, and she candidly opened her heart to me. She had many of the same questions as I did after 9/11: *Why did this happen to me? Why did God allow it? How am I going to get through the rest of my life without my husband?* Then she allowed me to open my heart to her, as I told her about my own spiritual journey (the condensed version) and shared some of God's promises. *He loves you. He promises to provide for you (starting with that life insurance). He promises to give you peace and comfort when you seek Him. And He promises to give you eternal life if you trust His Son Jesus Christ.* And in her eyes I saw that familiar glimmer of hope.

I believe that one of my callings is to be a notary for Jesus. Then again, I'm not alone. The Great Commission calls for *all* believers to be notaries for Jesus. Our job is to testify that He is who He says He is, and that He is the Person who gave the signature of His life on a binding contract for the forgiveness of our sins. "He who has received His testimony has set his seal to this, that God is true" (JOHN 3:33). But our job as notaries for Jesus is also to testify of His goodness and faithfulness to those who may believe otherwise.

Over the years since 9/11, I have had so many encounters with people who are going through a serious life crisis. They have experienced unthinkable tragedy and are suffering the pain and heartache of grief. They endure long illnesses with no relief in sight. They are in financial hardship with no light at the end of the tunnel. They have lost their loved ones... their homes... their income... their health... their independence... their dreams... and sometimes, they've lost their faith in God.

Though our circumstances may be very different, they share many of the same emotions that I did right after losing Jim.

They feel let down by God. They feel betrayed by Him. Disappointed with Him. Angry with Him. After all, if there really is a God, how could He let this happen?

Some of them come from a spiritually immature or biblically illiterate background, as I did. That usually explains why they question God's presence in the midst of their suffering, just like I did. Their ignorance and shortsightedness is what causes them to misunderstand God's nature and His character and His promises. My intention here is not to minimize their pain or to harshly criticize them, but to gently point out what was missing in my own life and what is missing in theirs: the knowledge of God through the power of His Word and a personal relationship with His Son.

I've also talked to veteran Christians when they feel like the world has bottomed out from under them. Though they usually don't question the existence of God, they do sometimes doubt the wisdom of God's plan. Perhaps they mistakenly assume that their years of faithfulness to the Lord should have made them exempt from suffering. Or maybe they believe that God has simply given up on them and they're on their own in the wilderness. In times of testing and temptation, even committed believers can find it challenging to trust God's goodness.

As one who has been through the refiner's fire, God has equipped me to notarize His faithfulness in times of adversity. I can testify firsthand to God's grace and mercy, His power and sovereignty, and His goodness and trustworthiness. Like Jeremiah, I can sign my name and set my seal on the truth that "the LORD's lovingkindnesses indeed never cease, for His compassions never fail, they are new every morning; great is Your faithfulness" (LAM. 3:22-23).

Conversely, as believers, Jesus is our notary. I see that so clearly as I read Jesus' beautiful prayer to His Father in John chapter 17 where He "notarizes" us. He witnesses on our behalf that we are who we say we are, and He identifies us as His followers, His disciples, His children. At Pentecost and at our own spiritual rebirth, He set His seal upon us in the form of the Holy Spirit. Paul told the Ephesian church: "In Him you also trusted, after you heard the word of truth, the gospel of your salvation, in whom also, having believed, you were sealed with the Holy Spirit of promise, who is the guarantee of our inheritance, until the redemption of the purchased possession, to the praise of His glory" (EPH. 1:13-14, NKJV).

I love the part that says, "you were sealed with the Holy Spirit of promise." The official seal of a notary is a large, round, indelible mark deeply embossed in paper. There is no way it can be altered without obvious signs of tampering. It is permanent and unchangeable and it authenticates the document. In a similar way, God "sets the seal" of His Spirit on the hearts of believers in order to guarantee and preserve our status: I BELONG TO GOD. Paul reminded young Timothy, "The firm foundation of God stands, having this seal, 'The Lord knows those who are His...'" (2 TIM. 2:18-19). Paul also told the Ephesians about "the Holy Spirit of God, by whom you were sealed for the day of redemption" (EPH. 4:30). And in the book of Revelation, John tells us that as believers, we will be with Jesus in Heaven and "His name will be on our foreheads" (REV. 22:4). Now that's a permanent embossing I can't wait to display.

·tf·

He who is faithful in a very little thing is faithful also in much;
and he who is unrighteous in a very little thing is unrighteous also in much.
Therefore, if you have not been faithful in the use of unrighteous wealth,
who will entrust the true riches to you?

~Luke 16:10-11

Cubic
Zirconia

12

Soon after we were married, Jim and I went shopping for a new queen-size mattress for our bed. After weeks of testing every mattress in the state of New Jersey, we finally found one that we both agreed upon — not too soft for him, not too firm for me. The display model was heavily discounted, but we didn't want a mattress that everyone else had been laying on. We were willing to pay the full price to guarantee that we'd get a brand new mattress. The salesman wrote up the order and assured us we would have a brand new mattress delivered to our home next Tuesday.

As we were leaving the store, Jim quietly asked me for a pen.

"Huh? Why do you need..." I answered as I shuffled through the contents of my purse to find one.

"Just hurry up and give me a pen," Jim muttered as his eyes scanned for the salesman, who was already busy helping another customer. I finally found one and handed it to him. He casually walked over to the display model of the mattress we had chosen. On the manufacturer's label that was sewn into the mattress, Jim used the blue ball-point pen to mark four small stars — one in each corner of the label. He "set the seal" in that mattress as a permanent way of branding it and distinguishing it from others. He did it so quickly and discreetly that the salesman didn't even know we were still in the store.

Tuesday came and so did our mattress, wrapped tightly in plastic and boasting a warehouse "new inventory" tag. The deliverymen carried it upstairs to our bedroom, unwrapped it, and placed it on our bed frame. Jim and I took one look at the mattress's sewn-in label and gasped — there it was, the star-spangled banner. We had been deceived. We had paid the full retail price for a deeply discounted display mattress. By the time I could utter a word, Jim was already on the phone with the manager of the mattress store. Someone got in BIG trouble. We later found out that the salesman had pocketed the $350 difference between the display model and the new inventory. "The acquisition of treasure by a lying tongue is a fleeting vapor, the pursuit of death" (PROV. 21:6). No, the salesman wasn't assassinated for his unethical business practices, but he is no longer employed by that company.

A few thousand years before the mattress incident, another deceitful swap took place. Jacob loved Rachel from the moment he saw her. On the day they first met, Jacob kissed her and wept for joy — he knew he'd met his soul mate. His life companion. His treasure. Rachel was the one, and he'd do anything to claim her as his wife. So he agreed to work for Laban, Rachel's dad, for seven years in order to marry her.

Seven years passed — a long time, yes — but when you're in love, you don't look at the clock. Finally, the wedding day came and so did the traditional conjugal activities. Jacob said "I do," went in to his new bride, and consummated the marriage. But in the morning, Jacob was horrified to discover that his father-in-law had tricked him. It wasn't Rachel in the bed, it was her older (and apparently less attractive) sister, Leah. Imagine the shocked look on Jacob's face — I'm quite sure the honeymoon was promptly over. It was a custom back then (whether Jacob knew about it or not) for the older daughter to be married first; and in spite of their agreement seven years before, Laban had deceived

Jacob into marrying Leah instead of Rachel. Jacob did eventually marry Rachel, but only after agreeing to serve Laban for another seven years. It's all there in chapter 29 of Genesis.

But before we shed any tears over poor Jacob, the victim of manipulation, rewind to chapter 27 and see how well Jacob also played the role of a con artist. With a little help from devious mother, Rebekah, Jacob pulled a fast one on dying father Isaac and stole the family blessing from older brother, Esau. The first-born son was entitled to the family blessing, which provided his inheritance and the honor of becoming the family's leader after the father died. Jacob took full advantage of Esau's temporary absence and his dad's poor eyesight, and he tricked Isaac into believing that he was really Esau. (He later got a dose of his own medicine with the Leah scam.) Anyway, the family blessing went to Jacob instead of Esau. The deal was done. It was official and irrevocable.

But before we shed any tears over poor Esau, the victim of deception, rewind two more chapters to Genesis 25 and see the apathy and disregard Esau had for his own birthright. Esau was hungry after a day's work, and Jacob had cooked some really tasty stew. Esau wanted some of that stew so badly that he agreed to trade his birthright for it. Esau got a plate of meat; Jacob got a double-portion of the family inheritance. There was no deceit involved, but it was far from an even exchange.

Here's the bad news: things are not always as they appear, whether it's a mattress or a sister or a brother. You've probably seen those fake Rolex watches that are virtually indistinguishable from the real thing; it's not until you closely examine them that you see the differences. (Okay, I confess. I own a counterfeit Coach handbag. I just can't justify the exorbitant cost for the real thing.) Fiction can look or sound a lot like reality. Deception can closely resemble the truth.

So it is with the teachings of God's Word. There are spiritual knock-offs and we need to be able to discern the real treasure from the cheap imitation. The only way to do that is to become so familiar with the truth in the Bible that we'll be able to recognize the falsehood when we see it. Unfortunately, not all counterfeits are as easy to identify as Jacob or Leah or that display mattress. Still, the Bible thunders with warnings about false teachers and distortions of the gospel; many people on the listening end want to have their ears tickled, so they turn away from the truth and turn to myths (2 TIM. 4:3-4). It's our responsibility to test everything we see and hear against Scripture. It's our responsibility to be a Berean. And if you don't know how a Berean behaves, you'll have to read Acts 17:11 or wait till the end of this book to find out more about them.

But here's the great news: things are not always as they appear. And so it is with God Himself. Sometimes it appears as if God had taken the day off when disaster strikes. It may seem as if God's plan was flawed when our country was attacked by terrorists. It may look as though God doesn't care if we're diagnosed with cancer. Unthinkable circumstances may give the impression that God is absent. But the truth is, nothing could be further from the truth.

Things are not always as they appear, and God proves that to me every day. Actually, He doesn't need to prove anything — but with His grace He gently shows me that I can always trust Him no matter what. Even when my world bottoms out, God is faithful. Even when I'm unfaithful, God remains faithful. Even when others deceive me, God remains faithful. Even when the earthly evidence suggests otherwise, God remains faithful.

·tf·

...I collected for myself silver and gold and the treasure of kings and provinces... I became great and increased more than all who preceded me in Jerusalem... Thus I considered all my activities which my hands had done and the labor which I had exerted, and behold all was vanity and striving after the wind and there was no profit under the sun.

~Ecclesiastes 2:4-11

Treasures
in Heaven

13

While sitting in my doctor's office, I thumbed through a popular, secular magazine. Rarely do I ever read secular magazines anymore, but I had already been waiting an hour (you know the story) and the boredom had gotten the best of me. I read an article titled "What Makes Us Happy?" and the writer listed the top ten according to her research. Here they are, in no particular order: beauty, money, education, youth, intelligence, free time, narcissism, social skills, job security, and last but not least: a sense of humor.

I wasn't laughing. God was noticeably absent.

If that wasn't disturbing enough, the writer also threw this in: "Surprisingly, religion didn't make the cut. Churchgoers who were interviewed said they enjoy going to church but they only get a small lift from the Lord."

A few minutes later I was called into the examining room. When the nurse tried to take my blood pressure, the cuff exploded.

I didn't know who to pity more — the writer herself, the oblivious fools who supplied the top ten, or the misaligned churchgoers. If they aren't experiencing the joy of the Lord, they're either in the wrong church or they're playing for the wrong team.

Why do people cling to what they can't keep and reject what they can't lose? I should ask myself that question because I was one of them not too long ago. We live in a culture that has made veritable gods out of money, recognition, and success. But one day we will leave behind everything we acquire — our finances, our possessions, our education and degrees — since everything this world considers treasure will be worthless in eternity. We think they will satisfy us, and they might for a while — but not forever. We won't need them in heaven, and they cannot save us from hell. Jesus said, "For what does it profit a man to gain the whole world, and forfeit his soul?" (MARK 8:36). He also said, "Do not store up for yourselves treasures on earth, where moth and rust destroy and where thieves break in and steal. But store up for yourselves treasures in heaven, where neither moth nor rust destroys and where thieves do not break in or steal; for where your treasure is, there your heart will be also" (MATT. 6:19-21).

Don't misunderstand. God gives us blessings upon blessings and gifts upon gifts to enjoy while we're in this world. There's nothing wrong with wearing designer clothes, driving a cool car, and dining in gourmet restaurants, as long as we always acknowledge Who they came from and we don't center our lives around them. According to 1 Timothy 6:17, God "richly supplies us with all things to enjoy," so we should never fail to put Him first and thank Him for His lovingkindness and generosity.

But let's go back to the question of why people cling to what they can't keep. I have to really examine my heart and be candidly honest with myself. Am I truly willing to relinquish the earthly treasures that God has graciously provided to me? Am I so attached to my gifts and blessings that I cannot imagine life without them? If God's perfect and sovereign plan requires me to lose something precious (again), am I willing to go along with it?

God gave me an amazing husband — the love of my life — but I had to accept losing him. At first I furiously protested it and blamed God for it, but eventually I came to understand that Jim was God's property — not mine — and He had the right to take Jim back. Now that I have a much greater understanding of the ways, the will, and the Word of God, can I accept losing another loved one without throwing an explosive tantrum? Am I willing to lose whoever or whatever God chooses to remove from my life? Am I willing to lose a breast from cancer? Or worse, am I willing to lose an arm or a leg (or both) from an accident? Am I willing to lose my entire savings account from medical bills or a stock market crash? Am I willing to lose my job? My house? Am I willing to part with any or all of my earthly treasures? I think of Joni Eareckson Tada and the late Christopher Reeve. Tragic accidents made them quadriplegics and radically changed every aspect of their lives. When I say, "Thy will be done," do I really mean it?

When I was speaking on this subject at a women's retreat, a young girl came up to me after a session. Her eyes were teary and she said, "When you talked about putting more emphasis on other people or things instead of God and you asked who or what sits on the throne of our heart... well, I realized that my Blackberry sits on the throne. My Blackberry is my god. I started thinking about how much I use it during the day... I even keep it on my nightstand when I go to sleep. And as soon as I hit the alarm in the morning, I grab the Blackberry and start checking my e-mail before I even get out of bed. I read the Bible once in a while, but I admit that I'd be really lost without my Blackberry. It has taken over my life and I can't live without it."

This poor girl fell for one of Satan's tactics — using technology to lure us into godless oblivion. We cried together, we prayed together, and we praised God for opening her eyes. I told her, "God isn't saying you can't have a Blackberry. He's saying, 'I want to trade places with that Blackberry.'"

God searches our heart and looks for that willingness to part with things and people we cherish, and He looks for our understanding that it all belongs to Him anyway. I think of how God asked Abraham to sacrifice his son Isaac as an offering to the Lord—a radical test of faithfulness and obedience (see Genesis chapter 22). Abraham's willingness to go through with it was all that God needed to see, and He aborted the mission just as Abraham's knife was poised and ready to strike. Perhaps my encounter with breast cancer was also a test for my willingness to give up certain treasures in my life.

During my radiation treatments, my hair mysteriously started falling out at an alarming rate. (Radiation doesn't normally cause hair loss unless your head is the area being treated.) I know I complain about my hair a lot, but I'd really like to keep it. At first I tried reasoning with God. *Lord, if having breast cancer means I have to lose something, I think I'd rather lose my breast than my hair. At least no one (except You and my doctors) will see that, but losing my hair is another story.* Call me proud or pompous or pitiful, but that was my logic at the time. Then I had the sobering thought that so many people in this world have lost far more than their hair, and I rebuked my selfish vanity. I reminded myself that God was in control, so I kept telling Him that I trust His outcome. "*I trust You, Lord. I know You have every hair on my head counted, so You know how much I've already lost. Thy will be done, Lord.*" I still struggled with "Thy will be done" every time I saw a fistful of hair in the drain, but I soon discovered the "What if—Then God" technique. Here's how that works:

What if I lose all my hair and it doesn't grow back? *Then God* will provide me with a wig and maybe I'll even like that hair better than my real hair. *What if* I ever become seriously disabled, unable to work and can't pay my bills? *Then God* will provide income for me in some other way. *What if* I lose another loved one? *Then God* will comfort me with His love and peace, just like He did when I lost Jim. *What if* this book never gets published? *Then God* will use the material for my speaking events. *What if* there are no more speaking events? *Then God* will give me a different way to serve Him. The "What If — Then God" technique has never failed me because God has never failed me. He promises to supply all my needs according to His riches in glory in Christ Jesus (PHIL. 4:19). He is Jehovah Jireh — the LORD who provides.

Job's words, spoken during the turmoil of grief and loss, also resonate in my heart: "The LORD gave and the LORD has taken away. Blessed be the name of the LORD" (JOB 1:21). That powerful passage of Scripture has been turned into a worship song — one of my favorites. In fact, I like it so much that I made it the ring tone on my cell phone. So every time my cell phone rings, I should be reminded that God has the power to give me earthly treasures, and He has the power to take them away. I often wonder how we ever lived without cell phones back in the day. Can I live without one now, if I had to?

Can I, like Job, trust that even if the earthly treasures in my life were taken away, I'd still have God? Can I sincerely bless the name of the Lord when something (or everything) of great value is taken from me? Can you? We don't always understand why God does what He does, but we know His ways are best. Paul said (with exclamation points, no less), "Oh, the depth of the riches both of the wisdom and knowledge of God! How unsearchable are His judgments and unfathomable are His ways!" (ROM. 11:33). Every treasure is from God. Or as James put it, "Every good thing given and every perfect gift is from above... from the Father of lights" (JAMES 1:17). I admit that I still sometimes catch myself in an attitude of entitlement, and that's when I need that spam filter again.

One of my favorite Proverbs says, "Give me neither poverty nor riches; feed me with the food that is my portion, that I may not be full and deny You and say 'Who is the LORD?' or that I may not be found in want and steal and profane the name of my

God" (PROV. 30:8). I believe that September 11, Hurricane Ivan (which destroyed Jim's underwater memorial), and my battle with breast cancer were all tests. They tested my ability to surrender to God's will, and they continue to test my level of contentment with what I have — not wanting more, and willing to accept less.

Paul certainly knew about contentment. From a Roman prison, he wrote, "I have learned to be content in whatever circumstances I am. I know how to get along with humble means, and I also know how to live in prosperity; in any and every circumstance I have learned the secret of being filled and going hungry, both of having abundance and suffering need. I can do all things through Him who strengthens me" (PHIL. 4:11-13). Paul knew how to be satisfied with a lot or a little. The secret was relying on God's promises and Christ's power.

When I follow Paul's example and look at my life through a lens of contentment and gratitude, my priorities fall into place. I detach myself from temporal treasures and I focus instead on eternal treasures. And the one treasure I don't ever have to worry about losing is my salvation through faith in Jesus Christ. Nothing can ever take that away from me — *not* nobody, *not* no how. I might lose my loved ones, but I can never lose God's love. I might lose my hair or my health or my house, but I can never lose heaven. I might lose my jewels or my job, but I can never lose Jesus.

·tf·

The kingdom of heaven is like a treasure hidden in a field, which a man found and hid again; and from joy over it he goes and sells all that he has and buys that field.

~Matthew 13:44

Buried
Treasure

14

Charlemagne,
king of the Franks and an emperor of Rome, was a powerful
leader in the late eighth century A.D. Also known as Charles the
Great, this guy was a bigwig in his time. Dignified, authoritative,
and ridiculously wealthy, he conquered many kingdoms and
greatly influenced the religious and political history of Western
Europe. Legend has it that hundreds of years after his death, his
tomb was discovered and opened, and his body was found in the
exact state that he had meticulously instructed in his final requests. Though his flesh had fully decomposed, Charlemagne's
skeleton was found in the vault, sitting upon a throne. He had
been fully dressed in royal purple with a crown on his skull, a
scepter in his hand, a sword by his side and an open Bible on his
knees. And one bony finger pointed to Mark 8: 36-37: "For what
will it profit a man if he gains the whole world, and loses his
own soul? Or what will a man give in exchange for his soul?"

Imagine what a sight that would've been for the archaeologists who excavated the tomb. If that didn't serve as their spiritual alarm clock, then I don't know what could. Whether or not
the details in this story are totally accurate, it still paints a clear
picture of the biblical truth that lies behind it: when we leave
this world, we leave all our earthly treasures behind. After that,

we'll either be spiritually alive and rich, or spiritually dead and poor.

By the early 1900s, J.P. Morgan was another ridiculously wealthy guy. He had built a financial empire that would have your head spinning. At the time of his death, his estate was worth 68 million dollars (about 1.4 billion in today's dollars). His fortune was the result of founding and acquiring and consolidating and investing in banks and railroads and art collections and electric companies. He bailed out the U.S. government in 1893 when the Treasury almost ran out of gold. His house on Madison Avenue was the first electrically lit residence in New York. He even had a gemstone ("Morganite") named in his honor. He was the Bill Gates of the Industrial Revolution.

If your head isn't spinning yet, then you haven't read his last will and testament. It was longer than some of his railroads and contained more financial transactions than most of us carry out in a lifetime. Nevertheless, in that legal document, J.P. Morgan clearly stated what he considered to be his greatest investment:

> *I commit my soul into the hands of my Savior, in full confidence that, having redeemed and washed it in His most precious blood, He will present it faultless before my heavenly Father; and I entreat my children to maintain and defend, at all hazard and at any cost of personal sacrifice, the blessed doctrine of the complete atonement for sin through the blood of Jesus Christ, once offered, and through that alone.*[4]

By the way, Morgan had been scheduled to travel on the maiden voyage of the *RMS Titanic* in 1912, but he cancelled his trip at the last minute. I'd say *that* was a wise decision.

Morgan knew he couldn't take his fortune along on his trip
to eternity, and he knew how important it was to leave behind a
godly legacy to his kids. Charlemagne testified that our real treasure lies in heaven, and he left behind a dramatic illustration to
prove the point. I don't have the wealth that J.P. Morgan had and
I won't be using Charlemagne's drastic measures, but will my
own personal testimony still have an impact in God's kingdom?
I wonder if the lives of J.P. Morgan and Charlemagne reflected a
commitment to Christ as much as their deaths did, and I wonder if my own life will be remembered more than my death. Paul
wrote,

> *Instruct those who are rich in this present world
> not to be conceited or to fix their hope on the
> uncertainty of riches, but on God, who richly
> supplies us with all things to enjoy. Instruct
> them to do good, to be rich in good works, to be
> generous and ready to share, storing up for
> themselves the treasure of a good foundation for
> the future, so that they may take hold of that
> which is life indeed.* (I TIM. 6:17-19)

At the end of
Paul's life, he was chained in a horrific Roman dungeon like a
criminal. Many years before, at Paul's conversion, Jesus appeared
to Ananias in a vision and told him the plans He had for Paul:
"He is a chosen instrument of Mine, to bear My name before the
Gentiles and kings and the sons of Israel; for I will show him
how much he must suffer for My name's sake" (ACTS 9:15-16).
And suffer he did, all for the sake of Christ. Paul had been heavily
persecuted, beaten, stoned, shipwrecked, and once again imprisoned — this time for good. He knew his work was done and his
life on earth was nearly over; and yet, remarkably, he was still able

to proclaim the gospel from the dungeon. Paul wrote his last let-
ters there as a final chance to tell Timothy about the things in life
that really matter. He wrote things like, "The love of money is a
root of all kinds of evil, for which some have strayed from the
faith in their greediness, and pierced themselves through with
many sorrows" (1 TIM. 6:10, NKJV). He warned Timothy to
"guard through the Holy Spirit who dwells in us, the treasure
which has been entrusted to you" (2 TIM. 1:14). And J.P. Morgan's
last will even reflected some of Paul's last words: "I know whom I
have believed and I am convinced that He is able to guard what I
have entrusted to Him until that day" (2 TIM. 1:12).

Paul and Charlemagne and J.P. Morgan all make me wonder
what I would say or write to my family and friends if I knew it
was going to be the last time I'd be able to communicate with
them. My words would seem so incredibly trite, but of course I'd
tell them how much I love them. I'd thank them for the tremendous role they played in leading me to Christ and strengthening
my walk with Him. I'd tell them how grateful I am that God put
them in my life. And to most of them, I'd be able to say, "Till we
meet again..."

But what will I leave behind to everyone else as a reminder of
my faith? Will people simply remember me as a 9/11 widow
who wrote a few books? Will my actions speak louder — and last
longer — than my words? I've been called a "Jesus freak" by *USA
Today* newspaper[5] — an accolade to those of us who know
Christ, but a mockery to those who don't. Is that how I'll be remembered? There was a time not too long ago when I was spiritually ignorant. I assumed that anyone who reads the Bible is a
Jesus freak, and I used that term with fully negative undertones.
But I pray that I can gently correct that shortsightedness when I
encounter it in other people. I pray that I can be an ambassador
for Christ, representing Him in the way He so rightly deserves. I
pray that I can leave His mark on the hearts and lives of those

around me, without coming off as a religious nut to those who just don't get it.

When Charlemagne died, he got all decked out in full imperial attire for the occasion. All glory and thanks to Jesus, when I die I'll be wearing a much different kind of royal wardrobe. This is how Isaiah describes it:

"I will rejoice greatly in the LORD, my soul will exult in my God; for He has clothed me with garments of salvation, He has wrapped me with a robe of righteousness, as a bridegroom decks himself with a garland, and as a bride adorns herself with her jewels" (ISA. 61:10). I look forward to the day when you and I will be standing together in heaven, dressed in our royal attire.

For just as we have many members in one body and all the members do not have the same function, so we, who are many, are one body in Christ, and individually members one of another.

~Romans 12:4-5

Diamond Rings
and O-Rings

15

Sadly, it was determined that the tragic Challenger disaster was caused by inexpensive o-rings that had lost their elasticity in the cold temperatures the morning of the launch. (O-rings are small, round, rubber gaskets that sit inside a groove to create a seal.) Without a simple, functioning o-ring to create the proper seal in an important joint, there was no barrier to the explosive gases.

As a scuba diver, I am very familiar with o-rings on air tanks; it is part of every diver's routine to check them before a dive. A defective or missing o-ring can cause air to leak from the tank, and losing air when you're sixty feet or more underwater is definitely not a good thing. Sure, those o-rings might appear tiny and insignificant. They're made of rubber and they only cost a few pennies. They're not glamorous, and when nothing goes wrong, they don't get much attention. But they sure do come in handy. They even save lives.

The quiet, supportive role that they play reminds me of the background workers in the body of Christ. God has arranged for each of us to have different spiritual gifts to be used for different purposes, all intended to function together like a well-oiled machine. Yes, some people are as visible as the space shuttle's solid rocket boosters: the pastors and deacons and worship leaders and TV evangelists. But many others work behind the scenes, like those little rubber o-rings: the missionaries and ushers and Sunday school teachers and the kitchen clean-up crew. Alas, we often take those o-rings for granted. We don't realize how much we depend on them until we no longer have them around. Those who appear to play a less important role are actually indispensable. Just try starting a car without a spark plug. Or digesting dairy products without an enzyme called lactose. Or launching the space shuttle on a chilly morning without a functional o-ring. Big doors swing on little hinges, right?

Paul wrote to the Corinthian believers about this, only instead of talking about air tanks and o-rings, he used body parts.

> *There are many members, but one body. And the eye cannot say to the hand, "I have no need of you"; or again the head to the feet, "I have no need of you." On the contrary, it is much truer that the members of the body which seem to be weaker are necessary; and those members of the body which we deem less honorable, on these we bestow more abundant honor, and our less presentable members become much more presentable, whereas our more presentable members have no need of it.* (1 COR. 12:20-24)

Perhaps the Corinthian believers needed a little reminder that their ordinary gifts were in fact extraordinary, and that they should be given full respect. Or maybe Paul needed to deflate the egos of those who thought that their attractive gifts were far superior and were looking for recognition and honor. Whatever the case, Paul got the point across: every church member is important and necessary. If one part is taken away, the whole body becomes less effective. God treasures each individual, and each individual is worthy of honor. God uses our diversity to create unity.

I guarantee that Jim never thought his amateur talent for underwater photography would ever be used to advance God's kingdom. I'm sure he presumed that his treasured photographs would go no further than the shadow boxes that house them. But God knew exactly what He was going to do with those photos long before Jim even snapped the shots. After 9/11, I sent some of Jim's photos to the editor of his favorite scuba diving magazine, with the hope that they would do a tribute page to Jim. They did. One thing led to another, and it can now be said that God used a few pictures of tropical fish to bring forth a Christian writing and speaking ministry to spread the gospel message. (You can read about that amazing story in *Teachable*.) Big doors swing on little hinges, and rockets are launched with the help of a few o-rings.

Imagine Jesus sitting down in the temple in Jerusalem, casually observing the people as they made their tithes and offerings. Each one would step forward and drop their coins into the collection plate. *Clang. Clang-clang.* The more coins a person dropped, the louder the clangs. No doubt, some of the rich and famous were very proud of their big clangs. Others probably tossed their coins begrudgingly, making their clang with a heavy, aggravated sigh.

Then along came an old, destitute, Jewish widow. The Bible doesn't give a description, but I picture her all dressed in black with a few teeth missing, severe osteoporosis, and a bad limp (kind of like Yente the matchmaker in *Fiddler on the Roof*). She walked over to the collection plate and tossed in a mite. Her only mite. Her life savings. *Plink.* A mite by today's standards is worth only a fraction of a penny, equivalent to a paper clip or a thumb tack — or an o-ring. I wonder if anyone sneered or snickered at her. It was a pathetically meager offering in the eyes of everyone else around her... except for One.

Jesus knows our every thought, word, and deed. He is able to judge the thoughts and intentions of our heart. The widow's gift must have seemed so inconsequential to the onlookers, but to Jesus it was priceless treasure. He pointed out Yente to the disciples. "Truly I say to you, this poor widow put in more than all the contributors to the treasury; for they all put in out of their surplus, but she, out of her poverty, put in all she owned, all she had to live on" (MARK 12:43-44).

We often judge gifts and treasures by their physical size or their monetary worth. Most of us would prefer a mansion over a bungalow because we think bigger is better. And we'd usually choose a diamond ring over a refrigerator because the world tells us that good things come in small packages. But the value of a gift is not determined by its size or its dollar amount; it's determined by the spirit in which it is given. The widow gave everything she had — her only treasure — and Jesus recognized its enormous value. What mattered to Him back then (and what matters to Him today) is not the size of a gift. It's the motive behind giving it or using it.

God looks for a spirit of gratitude and generosity when we offer our money, our time, or our talents. Listen to how Paul says it: "For if willingness is there, the gift is acceptable according to what one has, not according to what he does not have" (2 COR. 8:12, NIV). Each of us has a treasure in our lives, which, if presented to God with a grateful spirit and a servant's heart, could bring forth a remarkable outcome. God loves a cheerful giver and He has an important use for every one of our gifts — whether we offer Him a diamond ring or an o-ring.

tf

For you know the grace of our Lord Jesus Christ, that though He was rich, yet for your sake He became poor, so that you through His poverty might become rich."

~2 Corinthians 8:9

Spreading the Wealth

16

During my cancer treatments, I made a practice of praying while beams of high-energy radiation waves were aimed and shot at the cancerous site. I asked God to help me focus on His promises instead of my health problems. I praised Him for giving us the skills and technology to fight our battles with disease. I asked Him to please use this big, loud machine to kill off all the cancer cells; and I asked him to protect my heart, lung, and ribs (which were in dangerously close proximity to the beams of radiation). I thanked Him for giving me an amazing family and church, all of whom immersed me in prayer and surrounded me with care. And while beams of radiation were penetrating my breast, God's peace was penetrating my heart.

I still marvel at that peace He gave me during those treatments and how He used them to bring me even closer to Him. I think about how frantic and hysterical I would have been if I were diagnosed with breast cancer before I became a believer. In those days, I was not equipped with the Word of God and I did not trust Christ with my life and future. I would have had an entirely different reaction to the diagnosis and the treatment, and it wouldn't have been pretty. Back then, even a sprained ankle was the apocalypse.

But the good news is that my battle with breast cancer appears to be over, God willing. Even better news is that during those seven weeks of radiation treatments, God gave me several opportunities to talk to other cancer patients and some of the oncology staff about Jesus. Like the day they were falling behind in their schedule and I had to get to work (at the pharmacy) right after my treatment. Another patient sitting next to me (I'll call him "Bob") offered to let me go before him since he wasn't in a rush and I was. I thanked him for being so kind and considerate.

He chuckled and replied, "Well, hey... who says you can't get to heaven by bein' a good person?!"

Bells and alarms were going off in my head and I had to physically restrain myself to calmly and gently and respectfully say, "Well... ahem... actually, *Jesus* says that... and the apostles Paul and John. It's in the Bible, stated very clearly, many times." And that started a whole big discussion that continued for a few weeks. Each morning, we'd sit in our hospital gowns talking about Jesus and the plan of salvation. I do not know whether or not Bob ever made a profession of faith in Christ. His treatments finished before mine and I never saw him again. But I still pray that while beams of radiation were penetrating Bob's cancerous prostate, seeds of faith in Christ were penetrating his needful heart.

My speaking ministry requires me to travel quite a bit — never could I have imagined I'd be spending so much time in airports, planes, and hotels. As a pharmacist since 1989, I assumed my base of operations would always be behind a tall counter in a drugstore, but God had other plans. Although the travels can be exhausting, I've been tremendously blessed to meet so many believers around the country and be encouraged by their faith. As I prepare for each event, I always pray that the Lord will guide and direct every detail and that He will open the hearts and minds of those who will attend. I often wonder if God is sending me to a specific location for a specific person who needs to hear my message, and once in a while He confirms that thought and reveals who that person is.

It's not always someone in the audience, as I tend to assume. After all, God's thoughts are not our thoughts and His ways are not our ways. I was once scheduled to do a women's retreat in the town where I live; but there was a problem with the facility, so the retreat was moved to a hotel in Lancaster, Pennsylvania — three hours away. I was disappointed that I had to drive a long distance when I could have just driven down the road, but God soon made me aware of why those plans needed to be changed.

After my first session, I gave an invitation to the ladies to accept Christ as their Lord and Savior. Little did I know that one of the hotel workers — a man named Fernando — had been listening in the back of the room. He went over to the women's ministry team afterwards and said that he wanted to invite Jesus into his heart. They prayed with him, and I thanked and praised God for sending me on a three-hour detour so Fernando could hear the gospel and respond to it.

Three hours is nothing. One time, God sent me all the way to Canada so I could share Christ with the passenger sitting next to me on the plane during the second leg of my trip. God even switched my seat at the last minute so I'd be right where He wanted me: sitting next to Ian.

I'd say Ian was in his early sixties — well dressed and well spoken, with a very slight British accent. It didn't take long for him to strike up a conversation with me. He told me he was heading home to Ontario after a visit with his son in the States. He talked a bit about his son's family and mentioned some of the fun activities they did together.

"How 'bout you?" he asked. "Are you traveling for business or pleasure?"

Might as well test the waters. "Well... both. I'm speaking at a church. My business is for God, and it's a pleasure to serve Him."

Ian chuckled. "Ohhh, okaaay." He had the window seat, and he turned to look out the window, probably trying to think of what to say next. He finally came up with something.

"So, what kind of things do you speak about?"

Well, Lord, I think You just opened the door. Now please help me to walk through it. I hesitated for a moment and took a small breath.

"Well, my husband was killed on September 11 in the World Trade Center, and even though I —"

"Ohhh, I'm *so* sorry." He stopped me in the middle of the sentence. "How awful... did he work in the towers, or...?"

"Yes, he worked for Cantor Fitzgerald on the 103rd floor of Tower One."

I've had this conversation with so many people that I've gotten good at predicting where it will go from here. If the person is from New York or New Jersey, they will immediately begin telling me about the person (or people) *they* knew who perished that day. If the person is from elsewhere in the country, they are usually stunned and they're still trying to process the fact that they're talking to a real, live, 9/11 widow. In either case, since September 11 was such a global tragedy and the whole world remembers exactly where they were when it happened, I usually have their full attention at this point.

Having Ian as a true captive audience worked in my favor. He couldn't really get up and walk away — he was trapped in the window seat of a commuter plane holding thirty people. All I had to do was gently work the conversation back over to God. And Ian did it for me.

"So is that why you're speaking at the church?"

"Yes. I speak at different churches and Christian conferences and retreats, telling my story about how God used 9/11 to bring me closer to Him, and how He — "

"So you're a Christian?" The tone of his voice was kind of flat. In my experience, this is where these conversations come to a fork in the road. When I answer yes, the other person will usually either want to talk about Jesus, or they will quickly change the subject.

"I am now. I wasn't before 9/11."

"Really." Ian nodded his head slowly. He looked out the window again. I waited a few moments for any further comments. None came. So I kept going.

"That's what it took to get my attention."

"Pretty harsh tactic, don't you think? I'll never understand it." Ian shook his head in frustration.

"What, you mean why it happened?"

"I mean, why God *let* it happen. If there really is a God... I just don't get it." He was still shaking his head.

"That's the same thing I said when my husband was killed," I paused here, just for the effect. "But I trust that God is going to explain it all to me one day."

Ian shifted in his seat, then looked me square in the eyes. "Look, I'm not a religious person..." *Good,* I thought, *neither am I.* "But I guess I'm curious. How can you have that kind of trust after what happened to you?"

I spent the next few minutes giving him a simplified version of my testimony. How bitter and angry I was with God after 9/11... how God sent many people into my life to help me turn that anger into trust... how I started to read the Bible... how it all started making sense...how I invited Jesus into my heart and how He gave me a new life. Ian listened patiently until I was done with my monologue. Then he finally spoke.

"So. Jesus." Ian was looking at the seat in front of him.

"Yes. Jesus."

91

Now he was looking at me, and he had a slight smirk. "What is it about Jesus that you find so appealing?" *Hmmm, I thought. A flight to Australia and back wouldn't be enough time to tell him why I adore You, Lord.*

"Oh, so many things... but I guess I can sum it up in one word. His *love*." I actually felt my cheeks blush and my heart race as I thought about Yeshua. I felt like I was in sixth grade again, when I had a crush on Scott Rogers.

"Well, I've done some research on all the different religions... not because I want to get involved in any of them, but I just find it intriguing. I checked out Buddhism and Islam and Judaism and Christianity —"

Now it's my turn to cut Ian off. "Have you ever read the Bible?"

"I've glanced through it a few times, but I can't say I've read it cover to cover."

Now it's my turn to ask some questions. "So, in your research, what did you learn about Jesus?" I really wanted to just blurt out God's plan of salvation and tell Ian how much he needs Christ, but I knew I needed to evaluate his understanding before I could proceed any further. *Meet him where he's at. Don't start talking about algebra if he hasn't gotten past fractions.*

Ian answered confidently. "Well, Christians believe He's God in human form, and He died on a cross for their sins." *Okay, cool so far.* "They...well, you... believe in the resurrection and all that." *And all that. Lord have mercy.*

"Yeah, that's right. And that's pretty much all *I* knew before 9/11."

"So there's more?"

"Well, yeah. There were things I didn't know and didn't understand, until I started reading the Bible —"

"See, that's one place where I have a problem. The Bible was written by ordinary men, not God. It's a mixture of fact and fiction, and it was written so long ago. It's tough to prove whatever facts might be in it..."

Lord, please give me patience and open Ian's mind to Your truth. "Actually, the Bible was written *by God through* men. And there are plenty of historical and non-biblical sources that support Scripture... and archeological discoveries... thousands of prophecies that have already been fulfilled... but it really comes down to believing that the Bible is the absolute truth simply because God *says* it is."

Ian just shrugged. He wasn't convinced. I didn't expect him to be. Yet.

"Do you mind if I show you something?" I said, rummaging through my carry-on bag stuffed under the seat in front of me. I didn't wait for his answer. I pulled out my cute little turquoise leather travel Bible and quickly turned to 2 Timothy 3:16 before he could protest. I read it out loud, while showing it to him at the same time — just in case he'd think I was making it up. "All Scripture is inspired by God and is profitable for teaching, for reproof, for correction, for training in righteousness; so that the man of God may be adequate and equipped for every good work." Then I flipped over to 2 Peter 1:21 and read that. "But know this first of all, that no prophecy of Scripture is a matter of one's own interpretation, for no prophecy was ever made by an act of human will, but men moved by the Holy Spirit spoken from God."

"See," I said. "It's not just a book with some cool stories about floods and defeating giants and feeding five thousand people with a few fish. It's much more exciting than that."

"Okay, but how accurate is it? You're saying that book is thousands of years old. They had to copy everything by hand, so it's likely there were many errors made along the way. How do you know that the words haven't been changed since then?" *A valid question.*

I explained to Ian about how seriously the scribes took their jobs. I told him about the discovery of the Dead Sea Scrolls and that when they were compared with our modern Hebrew texts, the differences were found to be few and insignificant. Then I grabbed a Continental Airlines barf bag from the pouch in the seat in front of me and scribbled this on it:

Can yoo undrstnad this sentnece thuough even it conttains erors a few?

I asked Ian to try to read it out loud. He did, no problem. So I said, "In that same way, Scripture still speaks for itself in spite of a few typos. Nothing can discredit the Bible's reliability or its message. God makes sure of that."

Ian chuckled. I noticed he did a lot of chuckling. I wasn't sure if his chuckles were based on amusement or nervousness or ridicule of my beliefs. But he chuckled almost every time I gave him an answer.

Then he said, "So, you didn't start reading the Bible until after 9/11? What made you start?"

I cleared my throat. "Well, I was looking for answers. I wanted to know why God allowed that to happen to me. And people were telling me about Jesus so I wanted to see if what they said was true. I found a lot of those answers, and I learned so much about myself..."

"Yourself?" There he goes chuckling again. "I thought you wanted to find out about Jesus."

Hold on to your hat, Ian, I'm gettin' there. "I did find out about Jesus, but first I had to understand something about myself. I realized how much I needed Him."

"Oh, you mean like, the forgiveness of sins?"

"Exactly."

"Now see, this is what gets me. Radical Islamic terrorists killed thousands of people — including your husband — and *you're* looking for forgiveness for *yourself.* Those insane murder-

94

ers are going to hell. I don't think *you* have to worry about going there."

"Well, I don't anymore... now that I've come to know Jesus as my Savior." *Okay, Lord, we're laying it all out on the table now.*

"So you're saying that you've done something so evil that you would've gone to hell for it?"

"I'm saying I realized I'm not the good person I thought I was. And yes, if it weren't for Jesus, I would've gone to hell for it."

Ian chuckled. I kept going.

"Okay, it's like this. If a person is diagnosed with cancer, the goal of the treatment is to destroy even the most microscopic cancer cells. If even one single cell is left over after surgery or chemotherapy or radiation, then technically, that person still has cancer. All it takes is one single cancerous cell to multiply and spread, right?"

Ian nodded. "Yeah..."

"Well, just like cancer cells, our sins can multiply and spread. Fortunately, most of us are not born with cancer. But we are all born as sinners — it's part of our DNA. We have cancer of the soul. It's the result of the fall of man and the genetics of original sin. We're sinners by nature and sinners by choice. You know about Adam and Eve?"

"I know the story. I'm not saying I believe it, but I know the story."

"So you believe in the evolution theory?"

Ian let out a long sigh. He rubbed his temple with his fingers and stretched out his legs. "I don't know what I believe, honestly. I want to believe in God. I really do. I want to believe there's a heaven... or some place a lot nicer than here. I want to believe that God created us and loves us. But with all the madness in this world, I have a hard time accepting that. What kind of a God sits back and lets the Holocaust happen... and earthquakes... and cancer... and 9/11... you know?"

95

I spoke as softly and gently as I could, over the hum of the plane's engine. "It's not God's fault that there's so much evil in the world. It's our fault for rebelling against Him in the first place. All the hatred and violence and sickness and despair we see — it's all a result of sin that we brought upon ourselves, with the help of Satan. Just because we aren't terrorists doesn't mean we don't have sin in our heart. We're far from perfect. Here, look."

I opened the Bible to Romans chapter 3. "Read verses 23 and 24, right there." I pointed to them.

Ian read it out loud. "For all have sinned and fall short of the glory of God... being justified as a gift by His grace through the redemption which is in Christ Jesus."

"Wait. Now read another." I flipped the pages to chapter 6. "Read verse 23."

"The wages of sin is death, but the free gift of God is eternal life in Christ Jesus our Lord." He paused. "I still don't see how this addresses my question of why God allows so much suffering in this world."

"Before you understand why God allows suffering, you have to understand the root of where that suffering came from. It resulted from sin. God allows suffering for many reasons — our flight isn't long enough to cover them all — but one reason is because there's work to be done in our hearts that can't be accomplished any other way. It's like what I was telling you before. God allowed my suffering on 9/11 because I had to learn about myself and what was missing in my life. I had to learn that I needed Jesus."

Ian paused for a few seconds, then spoke firmly. "The God I want to believe in is a loving God."

I practically jumped out of my seat. "Well, that's the same God I believe in — the one, true, living God who loves us more than we'll ever be able to comprehend!"

He continued, "But the God I want to believe in doesn't send good people like you and me to hell. He's fair."

I smiled softly and spoke as delicately as I could. "God *is* fair. And He doesn't send anyone to hell. We send ourselves to heaven or hell, as a result of the choice we make in this life — by choosing to either accept His Son Jesus, or by choosing to reject Him."

I paused and let Ian digest that for a few moments before I kept going.

"I think you're making the same mistake that I used to make. I was comparing my seemingly trivial sins with the rest of the world — you know, the murderers and rapists and terrorists — so I thought I was doing okay." I paused again. "If you take a bleached white sock and hold it up against a piece of black velvet, it looks really white and clean, right?"

Ian nodded. His eyes seemed to be fixed on my tray table.

"But if you take that same white sock and hold it up against freshly fallen snow, it looks dirty."

Ian didn't say anything. So I kept going.

"I never saw my sins through the eyes of a righteous, holy, perfect God. I saw my sins through the eyes of the rest of the world and I thought I looked pretty good. So I didn't think I needed Jesus. I thought I was doing just fine on my own. I knew I wasn't perfect, but I used to think that if I did enough 'good' things, they would compensate for the 'bad' things."

"Yeah," Ian chimed in, chuckling of course. "I've heard that philosophy before."

"But that would be like if I was on a diet and I ate a hot-fudge sundae. Then right after that, I ate two pounds of broccoli as if somehow they'll cancel each other out. The fact is, I still ate the hot fudge sundae. I'm still guilty."

This time, Ian gave me a hearty laugh. "Are you saying that ice cream is a sin? If so, I'm really in trouble."

I laughed with him. "Nooo... In fact, I'm confident that there will be an eternal supply of Ben and Jerry's in heaven. And fat, calories, cholesterol and diabetes won't ever be an issue."

"Well that's encouraging."

"Yeah. But that's only in heaven, and no one can enter heaven as a sinner. Not even with an *almost*-flawless record. Even if one single cancer cell is in my body, then I have cancer, right? Even if one single sin is in my life, then I'm a sinner. God has really high standards, and He won't negotiate or compromise them for anyone."

Ian said, "See, I don't think that's fair."

"But it *is* fair. If heaven isn't perfect, then why would we want to go there? We already live in a broken world. When we die, why would we want to go to another place that's the same as where we are now? Would you want heaven to be filled with people who lie and cheat and steal and use profanity?"

"Well no, but —"

"Or people who criticize and gossip about you? And people who get mad when things don't go their way? If God didn't demand perfection in heaven, there wouldn't be any distinction between earth, heaven, and hell. They'd all be miserable."

"So if you're right and we're all sinners, then no one is in heaven."

I pointed to Romans 6:23 again. "Like it says, the penalty we pay for our sins is death — permanent separation from God. But remember the other half of that verse. 'But the free gift of God is eternal life in Christ Jesus our Lord.' See, God provided a solution. He sent Jesus to fix our biggest problem — sin — the one thing that keeps us out of heaven." I shifted in my seat to face Ian better. "Jesus is the living Son of God. He came here and lived a perfect, sinless life, then He offered *Himself* as a *substitute* for our sins. He was brutally executed on a cross, but then He was resurrected three days later. And the same power that resurrected Him will resurrect those who trust in Him. Jesus took what *we* deserved — death. And He gave us what we *don't* deserve — life. Now, is *that* fair?"

Ian said, "Well, it doesn't seem fair to Jesus."

98

"It wasn't. But it was done purely out of love for us. Now you see why His love is so appealing to me."

Ian smirked. He didn't say a word, and no chuckles. He just smirked. There was a long pause in the conversation — probably the longest one since we got on the plane. I wanted to let him process everything, but I was afraid he might change the subject. So I very gently spoke up.

"He went to the cross for you, too, ya know."

I can't be sure, but I think Ian rolled his eyes. *I'm not letting this go.*

"We don't deserve it. We don't deserve to go to heaven. We aren't entitled to it, and we can't earn it. The Bible says we are saved from hell by God's grace, when we have faith in Jesus Christ and Him alone."

This time *I* chuckled. "I used to think that 'grace' was just that short, little prayer that you say before you eat supper. But grace by definition is 'undeserved favor.' We definitely don't deserve God's favor. But Jesus made a loophole for us. Here, look."

I opened to Ephesians 2:8-9 and read it out loud while Ian followed along. "'For by grace you have been saved through faith; and that not of yourselves, it is the gift from God; not as a result of works, so that no one should boast.' See, it's a gift — it's free — from God. You don't pay someone for a gift, otherwise it wouldn't be a gift. Right?"

Ian nodded.

"But just like any gift, it only becomes ours when we accept it and take possession of it." I reached into my carry-on bag again and grabbed the only snack I had brought with me (and I was dying to eat it). "Here's a 3 Musketeers bar. Let's say I bought it for you. I really want you to have it. It's my gift to you." I opened Ian's tray table and put the candy bar on it.

He chuckled, of course, then he flippantly answered me. "I don't like 3 Musketeers, and I'm borderline diabetic. Thanks anyway."

The candy bar stayed right where I put it. Ian winked and grinned. I grinned back with a heavy sigh. I can't wink.

"Can you just *pretend* that this is one of your favorite snacks or something? Better yet, pretend it's something that has so much value we can't even put a price on it. I'm trying to give it to you — as a gift — but it's not yours unless you take possession of it. It's your choice. Take it or leave it."

The candy bar still sat there. Ian didn't touch it. He just chuckled. Big surprise.

"See, we all have an option of where we spend eternity — and it's our choice, not God's. He provides us with the choice, but He doesn't make it for us. He wants us to love Him sincerely, from our heart. You wouldn't want to force your son and his family to love you, would you?"

"No, of course not..."

"In the Bible, God says, 'I have set before you life and death... therefore, choose life.' And Jesus... is life." I showed Ian a few more verses like John 1:1 and John 1:14 and John 3:16 and John 14:6. I stayed in the book of John, hoping I wouldn't lose Ian's attention by turning too many pages. "Jesus gave His life for us, so that we could have eternal life through Him. So we can either accept His offer or reject Him. If no action is taken, then by default, we're rejecting Him. No decision is a decision. You either have cancer, or you don't. Jesus said, 'He who is not with Me is against Me.' It's that simple. And it's that incredibly awesome."

Ian looked at me — no chuckling this time — and his eyes were a little glassy. He looked at his watch — we'd be landing in a few minutes — then he cleared his throat and said, "You know, like I said before, I'm not a religious man. And usually when I get into these kinds of conversations with people, I end up telling them to leave me alone, I'm not interested. But this was different. It was actually enjoyable. And what you're saying... it makes sense... and you have such peace. I can't believe you have such peace after what happened to you."

"It's the peace that surpasses all understanding." I didn't bother referencing Philippians. "I don't understand why or how God does what He does, but the peace He gives me overpowers the need to know why it happened. And when I think about the extreme agony that Jesus went through to make sure I'd have that peace... well... it brings me to my knees."

Ian nodded slowly, then he looked out the window. I wanted to tell Ian about the sinner's prayer. I wanted to tell him about repentance and justification and propitiation and substitutionary atonement and sanctification. I wanted to tell him all about Jesus being the fulfillment of the Old Testament Messianic prophecies. I wanted to tell him that Jesus will be returning for the final judgment. I wanted to give him a full Bible study on the Trinity and the fall of man and Isaiah 53 and the Passover and Gethsemane and Calvary. I wanted to give him more explanations as to why God allows suffering. But the pilot made an announcement that we'd be landing in a few minutes. All portable electronic equipment must be turned off. Carry-on luggage must be stowed properly. Seat backs and tray tables must be returned to their original upright positions.

Ian's tray still had the 3 Musketeers on it. He picked up the candy bar in one hand and closed the tray with the other. "Mind if I take this with me?"

My heart was racing and I had to control how big I smiled. "I was hoping you would! But I thought you didn't like 3 Musketeers?"

"I'm acquiring a taste for it."

"*Really.*"

"I just want something to remember our conversation."

"I think a Bible would do a better job." I gestured with my Bible as I put my own tray away.

"I have one back home. It's very old. My grandmother gave it to me before she died."

"Cool..." I was still smiling as I put my Bible away and grabbed one of my ministry brochures with my website printed on it to give to him. "Please feel free to email me if you want to keep talking about this. Wait — let me write something on that."

On the empty back panel of the brochure I wrote:

To Ian

Thanks for keeping your heart and your mind open to hearing about Jesus! Enjoy that 3 Muske-teers — never forget what it cost. It was a blessing to meet you!

In Christ alone,
Jennifer Sands

And at the bottom, I wrote:

If you confess with your mouth Jesus as Lord, and believe in your heart that God raised Him from the dead, you will be saved; for with the heart a person believes, resulting in righteousness, and with the mouth he confesses, resulting in salvation. (Romans 10:9-10)

Ian thanked me. We parted ways as soon as we got off the plane. I went to shake his hand, but he gave me a hug instead. I never saw or heard from Ian again. But I pray for him.

Let me guess — you were hoping for an unmistakably victori-ous ending to this story. So was I. I wish I could tell you that Ian made a verbal profession of faith in Christ on that flight. I'm sorry if I disappointed you. The truth is, I don't know what was in Ian's heart since he never made it clear. He only used the metaphor with the candy bar, and I can't be sure of his true intentions.

For the record, our conversation was more extensive than the details I gave you. I had to squeeze a ninety-minute discussion into one chapter of a book. And of course, afterwards I thought of a hundred verses I should have shown him and a million things I should have said. Yes, our time was limited since it was a short flight, but I kick myself for not boldly asking Ian if he'd like to pray to receive Christ just before we landed. And I kick myself for not asking Ian for his e-mail address so I can check in with him once in a while. Then again, not all witnessing opportunities result in an immediate conversion. Many of them involve gardening rather than harvesting. God does not expect us to do it all. On the contrary, He asks us to simply share the gospel and let the Holy Spirit do the rest.

I thank God for sending me to Canada to meet Ian. I praise Him for opening Ian's mind to at least listen to me. And I trust that the Holy Spirit will continue to work in Ian's heart. With God, all things are possible. If He can use a terrorist attack on our country to bring forth my greatest treasure, He can certainly use a candy bar at 25,000 feet to bring forth Ian's.

O LORD, our Lord, how majestic is Your name in all the earth, who have displayed Your splendor above the heavens! When I consider Your heavens, the work of Your fingers, the moon and the stars, which You have ordained; What is man that You take thought of him, and the son of man that You care for him?"

~Psalm 8:1, 3-4

A Feast
for the Eyes

17

I'm almost embarrassed to admit this, but art is not one of my passions. I'm simply not interested in paintings. I don't know why; they just don't inspire me. I'm usually bored to tears in art museums. I've been to the Sistine Chapel and greatly admired Michelangelo's work, but I didn't leave there feeling much different than when I went in. I've seen original works by Monet and Van Gogh. They're very beautiful, but I really don't need to see them again. I mean no disrespect, but Picasso's paintings give me a headache.

Many years ago, Jim and I attended a scuba diving expo. Among many exhibitors was a young artist who was painting a picture of an underwater scene. As we walked by his booth, Jim slowed down to watch him paint. Normally I would've pulled Jim's arm to keep moving, but I noticed that the artist (Mark Hagan) was painstakingly working on the yellow scales of a queen angelfish, which happens to be my favorite tropical fish. As we watched, Mark meticulously, tenderly, and lovingly added each brushstroke to the painting. The fish seemed to be coming to life right before our eyes. It was mesmerizing.

Mark took a deep breath and stood back, cocked his head a bit, and examined his work. He looked over at us and grinned. Jim and I complimented him on his gift for capturing the beauty of marine life, and that prompted a long conversation, which started in the main aisle of the expo and ended an hour later over coffee and donuts. We exchanged diving stories, talked about our favorite islands, discussed marine preservation, and shared our future endeavors. By the time we were ready to leave, I would have paid any amount of money for that angelfish painting, but, unfortunately, it wasn't for sale.

For me, the difference between the famous Michelangelo and the unknown Mark Hagan is not their ability to create a masterpiece. It's the fact that I know one personally and the other I don't. Knowing the artist gives me a much greater appreciation and value for the art itself. It takes on a whole new perspective with a far deeper meaning.

This is why I now look at a beautiful sunset with tears running down my face as I marvel at what God painted in the sky for me. It's why I stand breathless on the beach, watching how He makes those powerful waves crash one upon another. It's why I'm so easily amused as I watch two squirrels playfully chasing each other back and forth across the fence in my yard. I know (I *yada*) their Creator personally, and that makes all the difference in the world. What once made me shrug my shoulders now makes me get down on my knees. What I once looked upon with indifference, I now consider invaluable. What used to keep me in a state of autonomy now puts me in a state of awe. Was blind, but now I see.

God's creations are complimentary samples — trial-size treasures — free glimpses of even more spectacular masterpieces that await us in heaven. So often we think of priceless treasures as magnificent displays of wealth — like a palace or bright, sparkling diamonds in a ring. But what could be more priceless than the natural beauty that God created to reveal His glory? Yes, some of God's creations are indeed palatial — like Niagra Falls or the Swiss Alps. But like o-rings, some of God's creations are

106

tiny treasures that initially appear to be inconsequential until we take a closer look. How often we're fooled by first impressions.

Consider the works of the LORD and His wonders in the deep. As scuba divers, Jim and I discovered that some of the most fascinating creatures were also the smallest and easiest to miss. The tiny, red, pistol shrimp gives you a bang for your buck (sorry for the pun). The size of a quarter, God gave them petite but powerful snapping claws to make loud, popping sounds, which scare off intruders and help them capture food. And when I say loud, I mean *loud*. They sound like a machine gun breaking the silence of the underwater world. The first time Jim and I saw and heard one, we were astounded. *That little thing is makin' all that noise?*

Did you ever wonder why fish eyes bulge out from the side of their head? It provides a panoramic field of vision that allows the fish to see almost completely behind them. God equipped them with front, side, and rear-view mirrors. (Are we missing out on something?) And have you wondered why some fish have bright and pretty horizontal lines on their bodies? God didn't design them just for aesthetics; the lines also serve a purpose. Schooling fish use both their panoramic vision and the horizontal lines to maintain their position within the group. It's amazing the way a school of fish will move in unison, as if they were being led by a single mind.

That sounds to me like the biblical description of the Body of Christ: moving in unison and being led by a single mind. In other words, maintaining our position by focusing on the lines of God's Word and being led by the Holy Spirit. Paul encouraged the Philippians to do that: "Make my joy complete by being of the same mind, maintaining the same love, united in spirit, intent on one purpose" (PHIL. 2:2). Not that God or Paul intended for us to be robots. Certainly not. But as believers, we should have a common attitude of working together, serving each other,

107

and following our Leader. Like a school of fish. That's not the real reason why the fish (icthus) is a Christian symbol, but I like the concept.

On vacation in St. Maarten a few years ago, I was sitting alone on a quiet beach in a lounge chair, reading a book and enjoying the sun. In the corner of my eye, I saw a fairly large crab poke his way through the sand right next to my chair. He was adorable. His protruding eyes looked around to see if the coast was clear, then one leg at a time he started to climb out of his hole, ready to make a beeline for the water. But then I shifted position to get a better look. The sound startled him so much that he dove back into the hole in a frenzy. A few minutes later, he tried again. This time I made sure I didn't move, but a breeze ruffled the pages of my book and again he scrambled back into the hole.

This went on all afternoon. Every time that crab tried to make a run for the water, the slightest noise would scare him and he ran for cover instead. At first it was entertaining, but after a while it was pathetic. The poor guy had a serious case of paranoia. I knew he wanted to get to the water, which was only about fifteen feet away — so close, yet so far. I just wanted to gently scoop him up and walk him down to the water, but he moved too fast. Besides, I'm sure he would have given me a good pinching with his claws in defense.

He didn't understand that not only was I was harmless, but I actually wanted to help him. As I watched his behavior all afternoon (I gave up on the book), I saw my own paranoid tendencies in that crab. We both share the same Creator, but I know Him personally and the crab doesn't. How much more, then, should I be trusting God to take care of me? In His Sermon on the Mount, Jesus said, "Look at the birds of the air, that they do not sow, nor reap nor gather into barns, and yet your heavenly Father feeds them. Are you not worth much more than they?"

(MATT. 6:26) So then, why would I ever let my fears get the better of me? God gave that crab an instinctive nature — he thought I was the enemy and his instincts told him to run. But I hold a much greater value than the crab. God gives me discernment (through His Word and through the Holy Spirit) to know when to run and when to trust and when to stand still and wait. And even though the journey may be rough at times, He gave His Son as a promise that I'll make it to the water safely.

All around me I see God's brilliance and awesome power displayed in His creations — from the tiny pistol shrimp in the sea to the natural granite countertop in my kitchen to the massive ball of fire in the sky. From the colorful queen angelfish to the Grand Canyon to the big, fat, full moon at night. My eyes have been opened to the beauty and wonder of creation, and I *yada* the Artist who made them all.

I will give you the treasures of darkness and hidden wealth of secret places, so that you may know that it is I, the LORD, the God of Israel, who calls you by your name.

~Isaiah 45:3

The Treasures of Darkness

18

The book *The Last Days of Pompeii* tells a story about a young girl who was blind from birth and was bitter about her handicap. Then Mount Vesuvius blew. Molten ash spewed out like a vast umbrella and completely blocked all the light. There was panic and chaos as the people tried desperately to escape. But the girl was able to calmly and easily guide herself and her family out of the city because she already knew her way around those streets in darkness. They were saved from certain death, and her handicap became a treasure.⁶ The story is fictional, but it points to the important and encouraging truth that God can use our difficulties, trials, and handicaps for good.

I love Bible stories like the one in 2 Kings 7, where God makes treasures out of handicaps. The Arameans were threatening to attack Samaria. Four starving, handicapped lepers weighed their options and realized they would surely die if they stayed where they were. So they decided to take the only chance they had: go over to their enemy, the Arameans, with the hope that they might actually show some compassion and give them food. Amazingly, the Arameans thought that the lepers were an army coming to attack so they dropped everything and took off.

(Only God can make four diseased and starving men sound like the Israeli Defense Force.) The lepers got on the buffet line and fixed themselves a nice dinner plate, put on some new clothes, and then went to tell the king of Israel about the enemy's evacuation. Their nation was saved from an attack, and their handicap became a treasure.

Corrie ten Boom spent many years in the Nazi concentration camp Ravensbruk, where she endured unthinkable conditions in the women's barracks, including the infestation of head and body lice. That in itself would have traumatized me, but in her book, *The Hiding Place*, Corrie said she was actually thankful for the lice. Why? Because the lice stopped the guards from going into those barracks, so Corrie was able to hold Bible studies with the other women. Who in the world would ever think that lice could become a treasure? Well, Corrie did, and so did God.

Then there was Tom Dempsey. He was born without toes on his right foot. A handicap? For most of us, yes, but Dempsey saw it as an asset and in 1970 he became the kicker for the New Orleans Saints football team. He once kicked a sixty-three-yard field goal — with half a foot — a record that still hasn't been broken as of the writing of this book. I can't even kick a football out of my backyard, and both of my feet are fully intact.

I think you get the point. With God's help, handicaps can turn into a treasure. But a treasure can also turn into a handicap. Remember King David's son Absalom? He made the headlines in 2 Samuel 14-18. Absalom had supermodel good looks and long hair, but he used the treasure of his attractive appearance to win over the people and start an insurrection against his father. Eventually it came down to Absalom's army against David's army, and David won. Absalom tried to escape on a mule, but his head got caught in a tree branch and the mule just kept on going. (You can't make this stuff up.) Absalom's handsome head was a treasure; but, ironically, in the end, it was his undoing.

All three synoptic Gospels tell the story of the rich, young ruler—a Donald Trump of the Holy Land—who asks Jesus, "What good thing shall I do that I may obtain eternal life?" When Jesus told him he needed to obey the commandments, the guy quickly claimed that indeed he does. Then he asked, "What am I still lacking?" Well, he surely didn't like the answer that Jesus gave him. "Sell your possessions and give to the poor, and you will have treasure in heaven; and come, follow Me" (MATT. 19:21).

The Donald's heart sank, and instead of following Jesus, he walked away from Him. No doubt he liked the sound of "treasure in heaven," but he wasn't ready to part with his treasure on earth yet. He claimed to have kept all the commandments, but in reality, he had violated the first and greatest one: You shall not have any other gods before Me (EXOD. 20:3). His wealth was his god, and he wasn't willing to give it up. There was nothing wrong with the fact that the rich, young ruler had money—it's no sin to be wealthy—but his love for the money and his reluctance to detach from it cost him the kingdom of God. His greatest treasure became his greatest handicap.

I bought an antique collectible from eBay—an original, full-page advertisement from a 1947 *Journal of the American Medical Association* (JAMA), a valuable medical resource, which is still highly respected today. The advertisement both fascinates me and shocks me when I read it. It pictures a distinguished-looking doctor wearing a lab coat with a stethoscope around his neck and a lit cigarette in his hands. The headline proudly proclaims, "More Doctors smoke Camels than any other cigarette!" The eerie words of R.J. Reynolds Tobacco Company went on to declare this: "It was their experience during the wartime shortage of cigarettes which taught people the big differences in cigarette quality. However, no matter how great the demand, we don't tamper with Camel quality. Only choice tobaccos, properly aged, blended, and unfiltered, are used in Camels."

Remember, this advertisement was in a medical journal. Sadly, many smokers discovered that their beloved cigarettes — endorsed by medical professionals — would eventually be proven to cause deadly lung cancer. Another treasure turned into a handicap.

As I write this chapter, I'm under a deadline and the clock is ticking. (In fact, it's ticking very loudly and I'm suppressing the urge to throw something at it.) Time is running out. *Time* — one of the most precious gifts that God gives us — can be a blessing or a curse, depending on what we do with it. Time is a treasure when I make the most of it, like when I lose a few pounds after making the time to exercise every day. But it's a handicap when I abuse it, like when I'm scrambling to get to work on time because I was lazy and got out of bed too late. (I recently fixed that recurring problem by taping Proverbs 6:9-11 to my alarm clock: "How long will you lie down, O sluggard? When will you arise from your sleep? A little sleep, a little slumber, a little folding of the hands to rest — and your poverty will come in like a vagabond." It worked.)

Spending quality time with the Lord is always a treasure, and I regret the thirty-eight years of my life when I foolishly ignored Him. *If only I could get that time back.* The six years I spent with Jim were a treasure. What I wouldn't do to have just sixty more seconds with him. *If only I could turn back the clocks.* Delays can become regrets and missed opportunities can become stumbling blocks. But instead of looking in the rearview mirror, I should be reaching forward to what lies ahead, pressing on toward the goal for the prize of the upward call of God in Christ Jesus (PHIL. 3:13-14). God has given us the precious treasure of time, but here's the handicap: we don't know how much we really have.

The Treasures of Darkness

I need not be reminded about how quickly life can change in the blink of an eye. The brevity of life should propel me into being a good steward of whatever precious time and other treasures I have, investing them wisely. All of us want to hear the Lord say these words: "Well done, good and faithful servant! You have been faithful with a few things; I will put you in charge of many things" (MATT. 25:21, NIV). But sometimes, in my ignorance or arrogance, I allow those treasures to go to waste and become handicaps. Jesus gives us this warning: "Whoever does not have, even what he has will be taken from him" (MATT. 25:29, NIV). Whether it's lice or leprosy... cigarettes or blindness... greed or good looks... toes or time... a curse can turn into a blessing, and vice versa. That's the reciprocity of treasures and handicaps.

Whew... I finished this chapter and made the deadline... with treasured time to spare.

There is precious treasure and oil in the dwelling of the wise,
but a foolish man swallows it up.

~Proverbs 21:20

Trophies

19

If you've read my first book, then you know that Jim and I were die-hard New York Giants football fans. I proudly remain one. And if you follow football, then you know that the Giants pulled off an unimaginable Superbowl victory in their 2007/2008 season and made history doing it. If you're neither a Giants fan nor a football fan, please continue reading anyway. There really are some biblical parallels and life lessons coming. I promise.

The Giants started out their 2007 season with a losing streak. After each game, the team was heavily criticized for their unstable performances — especially Coach Tom Coughlin and Quarterback Eli Manning. I confess that I was one of the many critics who insisted that both of them should be fired. Coach Coughlin couldn't make anything happen; and the only passes Eli completed were caught by the other team. (Okay, I exaggerate.) But toward the end of the season, all the pieces of the puzzle mysteriously fell into place and the team finally figured out how to play football. Right before our eyes, Eli transformed into a clone of his hugely successful quarterbacking brother, Peyton Manning.

Incredibly, the Giants won their way through the playoffs and made it into the Superbowl as underdogs — playing against the undefeated New England Patriots who were so convinced that they would clinch a history-making perfect 19-0 season that they had actually written a book about their presumed perfection. The book was scheduled to go to press the day after the Superbowl. But that didn't happen. Instead, the Giants played their hearts out and pulled off the victory in the last two minutes of the game. It was one of the most exciting games in the sport of football with spectacular plays that will age like fine wine.

Even if you're not a Giants fan, you have to be inspired by their perseverance and their teamwork. Even if you're not a Giants fan, you have to be inspired by a team who defied the odds and did what everyone said they could never do. Even if you're not a Giants fan, you have to be inspired by players like Ahmad Bradshaw and Domenik Hixon, who got down on their knees in the end zone to thank and praise God when they made touchdowns.

With that unbelievable Superbowl triumph, my family and I joined the other crazed Giants fans in the victory celebration. Television cameras captured the wild scene as the fans screamed and chanted, "Yeah! We won! We did it! We're the world champions!"

Don't you think it's funny how sports fans always use the phrase "*We* won! *We* did it!" when their team wins? When the USA wins a medal in the Olympics, we say, "*We* got the gold!" When our kid's team wins in little league, we say, "*We* won!" But "we" didn't win. The players and the athletes won. They did all the work; we just sat in the stands or on our sofa eating popcorn and cheering them on. *We* didn't win. Eli Manning threw great passes and David Tyree caught them on his helmet. Bonnie Blair broke records for speed skating and Michael Phelps won eight gold medals in swimming. *We* didn't do anything. *They* did everything. But because we are devoted fans, we can claim the victory with them.

And so it is with Jesus. He did everything. He led a perfect life and sacrificed it in an unthinkable challenge against a power-ful enemy — and He won. We did nothing to contribute to the triumph. We sat in the stands, our own lives imperfect and our own performances poor, while Jesus took the burden of every sin of the entire human race upon His shoulders. He fought the battle for us, and *He* won. Yet, by virtue of our identification with Him, we can say, "*We* won." Thanks be to God, who gives us the victory through our Lord Jesus Christ (1 COR. 15:57).

As I said, the Patriots were so convinced they would win the Superbowl that they had already written a book about their "perfect" season; but the Giants made sure that book never went to press. I have nothing against the Patriots, mind you, and I greatly respect their teamwork, skill, and athletic abilities. But there's nothing like seeing an underdog team with exceptional perseverance overcome the impossible. (Especially when your team is the underdog.)

Overcoming the impossible — now there's a concept that should be very familiar to us, since it's exactly what the Christian faith is all about. Original sin from the fall of man automatically makes us all underdogs against a diabolical enemy who would like nothing better than to publish a book about how he defeated us. But for those of us who trust in Christ's finished work on the cross, that book won't ever go to press. Instead, our names will appear in a different book — the book of life that Jesus Himself has written: "He who overcomes will thus be clothed in white garments; and I will not erase his name from the book of life, and I will con-fess his name before My Father and before His angels" (REV. 3:5). Who would not want to be on God's team?! "If anyone's name was not found written in the book of life, he was thrown into the lake of fire" (REV. 20:15). Who would ever want to be on Satan's team?! "... And they will bring the glory and the honor of the nations into it [the new Jerusalem]... but

119

only those whose names are written in the Lamb's book of life"
(REV. 21:26-27). By the blood of the Lamb, the underdog wins.
We win.

Owners and man-
agers of sports teams will pay an obscene amount of money to
secure athletes who will help them win the championship. If
you're the athlete being paid millions of dollars, then everyone is
watching you to see if you're really worth the investment. New
York Giants quarterback Eli Manning was under close scrutiny
as he played the 2007 season for a multimillion-dollar salary. In
the beginning of the season, Eli's performance made that figure
appear to be a huge mistake, but Eli was eventually redeemed
with a Superbowl win and a tremendous return on the team's
investment. Now I can proudly wear his #10 football jersey
without being ridiculed.

The apostle Paul reminds us that we were "bought at a price;
therefore glorify God in your body and in your spirit" (1 COR.
6:20, NKJV). Jesus purchased our freedom and salvation with the
price of His own life — and that should make me want to play
my heart out and go the extra mile for Him. So what kind of
return do I give Jesus on His investment? All too often I fumble
the ball. I run out-of-bounds. I'm guilty of personal fouls and
unsportsmanlike conduct. I try to play by the rules, but the penalties keep coming and I wonder why God doesn't just bench me
and shake His head and say, "How much did I pay for her?"

He doesn't bench me because He loves me with an everlasting love. Because when I confess those penalties, He is faithful
and just to forgive them. Because His mercies are new every
morning, so great is His faithfulness. Because in spite of my losing scores, I share Jesus' perfect winning record; so by His grace,
I can say, "We won!" I am a treasure to Him, and He is a treasure to me.

Trophies

In the 2007 season, the Giants had lost two significant players: Tiki Barber, who retired from the NFL after the previous season; and Jeremy Shockey, who broke his leg and was out for the remainder of the season. When Tiki announced he was retiring, we fans collectively grieved and mourned and wondered how we'd ever make it without him. When Jeremy Shockey was seriously injured, we again collectively grieved and mourned and wondered how we'd ever make it without him. The Giants endured the loss of two valuable players, and we fans couldn't help but throw our hands up in the air and say, "Well, there goes the season. We're done." But amazingly, the loss of those players made no difference in the end — and in fact, the Giants played even better without them. The team's commitment, growth, and perseverance made them stronger, and the end result was victory. Who woulda thought?

I look back on that first agonizing year after September 11 and I clearly remember thinking the same thing: *How will I ever live without Jim? My life is over. I'm done.* But sometimes when we face our greatest loss, God will bring forth our greatest gain. It's like Gideon and the battle at Midian (I'm so glad that rhymes so I can remember it). Gideon's army started out with 32,000 men; but God reduced the army to only 300 men so that Israel would know that the victory over the Midianites was by His power, not their own. Check it out in Judges chapter 7. Never could I have imagined that losing Jim would really not be the end of the game — on the contrary, that it would be the beginning of a new life with Christ and a ministry to serve Him. If we allow God to work in our lives, He is able to do far more abundantly beyond all that we ask or think, according to the power that works within us. (EPH. 3:20). All things are possible with God, because only He can take a tragedy and turn it into a victory.

Sports teams have a way of disappointing us fans. Just when we think they're going to pull off a championship, they blow it. The team might show great promise throughout the season, but so often they let us down in the end. There were many years before that 2008 Superbowl championship when the Giants finished the season on a pathetically embarrassing note, and I'm sure they will have more losing seasons in the future. They won't be alone. Every team does. No team or player is always perfect. Sooner or later, more often than not, every team will disappoint their fans.

Every team except the Trinity, of course. God the Father, God the Son, and God the Spirit hold the only continually perfect, unbeatable world record from the beginning of time to the end. Over and over, throughout history and in my own life, God has proven that "He will not fail you or forsake you" (DEUT. 31:6). Life on this side of eternity brings many failures, and I'm not just talking about sports teams. Our families disappoint us, our friends betray us, our co-workers reject us — and we do the same to them. But we can always count on the Lord because He always keeps His promises — even when we disappoint Him, betray Him, and reject Him. So "let us hold fast the confession of our hope without wavering, for He who promised is faithful" (HEB. 10:23). King Solomon said, "Not one word has failed of all His good promises" (1 KINGS 8:56, NIV), and Paul reminds us that "hope does not disappoint, because the love of God has been poured out within our hearts through the Holy Spirit who was given to us" (ROM. 5:5). That should make everyone want to play on God's team. With a record like His, we just can't lose. Only God can take a cross and turn it into a crown. Only God can take trash and turn it into a treasure. Only God can take a bad season and turn it into a Superbowl trophy. Yes, the players will disappoint, but the Coach never fails and the victory has already been determined. I can't say it any better than the bumper sticker on my friend's car:

"Final Score: Satan zero. God WON."

For what credit is there if, when you sin and are harshly treated, you endure it with patience? But if when you do what is right and suffer for it you patiently endure it, this finds favor with God.

~1 Peter 2:20

Stake Your Claim

20

It was a Saturday afternoon in the summer of 1997. Jim had just bought a new set of golf clubs, and off he went to the local driving range to try them out. I'm not a golfer so I planned to stay home. After Jim left, my sister, Maria, called to invite us for dinner that evening. I accepted. Since Jim was busy hitting golf balls, I decided I'd go to Maria's house for a dip in her pool and tell Jim to meet us there for dinner when he was finished. Maria's house is very close to the driving range, so it made better sense for Jim to head straight to her house instead of driving all the way back home first. I had to get in touch with him to tell him about our plans, but his cell phone was turned off. You know, golfer's etiquette.

So I called the driving range and explained the situation to the man who answered the phone. I described what Jim looked like and what he was wearing. I knew it was crowded with golfers that day, but I figured it wouldn't be too hard to find him — after all it's a driving range, not a golf course. All the man had to do was take a stroll down the field where all the golfers were lined up and look for the tall, thin guy with glasses, a maroon T-shirt, and khaki shorts and ask him to come to the phone.

After my brief explanation, I could hear the man exhale. It had a slight tinge of annoyance.

"What's his name?"

"Jim Sands."

I heard the man put the phone down, then I heard some bustling and clattering... then came a thundering voice over the loudspeaker: "JIM SANDS, COME TO THE FRONT OF-FICE, *YOUR WIFE* IS ON THE PHONE."

I think he used a megaphone with an amplifier. The words *your wife* were spoken with unmistakable sarcasm. I heard snickers from other guys in the office. So much for golf etiquette, and so much for my husband's ego. I knew I was in trouble.

A few decades later, Jim finally came to the phone. Even though he said only one single word, I could tell he was talking with his teeth clenched.

"What?"

"Uhhhh, sorry, hon... I really didn't think he'd do that... I thought he'd come find you... I, umm, I — "

"This better be important. What?"

"Just... go to my sister's house when you're done. We're having dinner there."

"*Well*, I'm done *now*."

That was my side of the story. Jim's perception was far more melodramatic:

"When that announcement was made, every guy in the place laughed and looked around to see who the henpecked husband was. I could hear the snide remarks: 'Your wife is on the phone!' and 'Who's on a leash?' and 'Better hurry home!' I was hitting all the way on the far side of the range, so I had to walk past twenty guys on my way to the office. I was mortified. I put my club down, put my head down, and took the walk of shame."

Bless his heart, Jim forgave me for crushing his ego and his new-golf-club euphoria. That story became legendary in our family. Every time Jim told it, it became more and more theatrical. We laughed about it for years. Jim never did return to that driving range.

The walk of shame. Have you seen it? Have you done it? I know I have. Just as Jim was a bit ashamed that day to claim me as his wife, there were times when I've been reluctant to acknowledge Jesus' claim on my life. Soon after my conversion, some former neighbors dropped by unannounced while I was reading my Bible. I quickly closed it and stuck it under a pillow. I knew where they stood with regard to religion — they wanted no part of it. I dreaded their looks... the remarks... the rejection... so I took the walk of shame and missed an opportunity to share my testimony with them.

Here's a scenario: let's say you're at work or school, surrounded by people who have no fear of (or belief in) God and consistently behave as if there won't be any consequences to their evil words and actions. A discussion arises that clearly profanes the very character of Christ. Do you speak up in His defense? Or do you take the walk of shame in the other direction? I've done both, and I'm ashamed of my walk of shame. You're in a restaurant having dinner with some old friends. The food comes and everyone's ready to dig in. If these were your church friends, you'd all pray first, but these are definitely not your church friends. Do you ask them to take a moment so you can give thanks for God's provision? Or do you take the walk of shame to the bathroom so you can pray privately? Or do you just forget about the prayer altogether?

I'm not saying that we should inundate our neighbors' mailboxes with gospel tracts and church literature. I'm not saying we should hold an office meeting to inform our co-workers that unless they repent, they're headed for Gehenna where there will be weeping and gnashing of teeth. There are appropriate times and places to share our faith and God's love. The aggressive, in-your-face approach usually backfires. Our testimony should make them want to know more, not push them away. And I'm not saying that we need to pray for a blessing every time we eat a bag of

127

chips or pop a stick of gum in our mouth. The Lord knows our heart and will see if we maintain a thankful attitude throughout the day.

But here's what Paul has to say: "I am not ashamed of the gospel, for it is the power of God for salvation to everyone who believes" (ROM. 1:16). Peter follows that with: "If you are reviled for the name of Christ, you are blessed, because the Spirit of glory and of God rests on you... if anyone suffers as a Christian, he is not to be ashamed, but is to glorify God in this name" (1 PET. 4:14, 16). In those two passages, the translation of *ashamed* means "embarrassed" or "to shrink away from." Interesting how one of those passages came from Paul, who, before his conversion, would've probably rather been a leper than be called an apostle of Jesus Christ. Even more interesting is that the other passage came from Peter, who swore he'd never deny Jesus, but he denied him three times just a few hours later. Fortunately for Paul and Peter and all believers, God's grace is more than a match for our shame and our guilt.

Jesus has the strongest words of all, directed at those who deliberately reject Him and refuse His gift of salvation: "Whoever is ashamed of Me and My words, the Son of Man will be ashamed of him when He comes in His glory" (LUKE 9:26). Jesus also said, "he who denies Me before men will be denied before the angels of God" (LUKE 12:9). Jesus Himself was rejected, humiliated, mocked, ridiculed, and put to death. He took the walk of shame — *our* shame — as He carried a cross down the Via Dolorosa on His way to Calvary. He took what we deserve — death — and He gave us what we don't deserve — life. Shame on us if we are ever ashamed of Him.

The writer of Hebrews says that God is not ashamed to be called our God (HEB. 11:16). Remember: we are His unique, versatile, durable, sentimental treasure. He places infinite value on us and is not ashamed to claim us as His children, even when

128

we misbehave. Even when we ignore Him or grieve Him. Even when we care more about what others think than what God thinks. So when I'm tempted to take the walk of shame, I pray that I will be ever mindful of the unique, versatile, durable, sentimental treasure that I have in God. And when He calls on me — whether it's a gentle nudging or a firm shove — I pray that I will drop whatever I'm doing and run to answer Him with a willing heart and my head held high.

You were not redeemed with perishable things like silver or gold from your futile way of life inherited from your forefathers, but with precious blood, as of a lamb unblemished and spotless, the blood of Christ.

~1 Peter 1:18

Ruby Red

21

On our trips to Israel, we always try to visit one of our favorite spots: Ben Yahuda Street in Jerusalem. It's a bustling, festive, pedestrian-only street lined with shops and restaurants and outdoor cafes. It is bursting with Jewish culture, illuminated with strands of white lights, alive with street musicians, and, as always in Jerusalem, patrolled by armed Israeli soldiers.

As you stroll along Ben Yahuda Street in the evening, you might be approached by a friendly (but overzealous) ultra-Orthodox Jewish gentleman who might attempt to tie a red string around your wrist, assuring you that it will provide deliverance and protection. (Of course, if he's successful with his pitch, he'll want a few shekels for the bracelet.) Both in Israel and here in the states, Orthodox Jews often wear "scarlet bracelets" to protect them from evil. In an orthodox Jewish community near where I live, some residents keep red ribbons in their cars as they drive, hanging off their rearview mirror — they won't leave home without it. Some traditions (actually, superstitions) even encourage Jewish brides to sew a small red thread into their wedding dress.

You may wonder, as I did, *what's up with the red string?* Well, it's all about Rahab.

Rahab's story takes place during the time of Joshua — somewhere around 1400 B.C. — a bloody and violent time for the Israelites. The place: Jericho. The people: a few Israeli spies on a mission to check out Jericho. The purpose: the Israelites needed to claim the land that God had promised them. The prostitute: Rahab.

For the record, most Bible translations describe Rahab as being a "harlot." The Hebrew word is *zanah*, which is usually translated as "prostitute." However, *zanah* can also mean "innkeeper," so we really should keep an open mind about what Rahab's choice of employment might have been. Whether she provided lodging or favors (or both) to her traveling customers, it wasn't Rahab's profession that counted — it was her faith in God.

Two of Rahab's hotel guests turned out to be Joshua's spies. She could have handed them over to the king; instead, she put her life on the line and secretly hid the spies. Rahab had heard about God's miraculous parting of the Red Sea and Israel's big victories over their enemies. Apparently, that was enough to convince her that the Lord alone is the one true God, and she shared her new-found belief with her new Israeli spy friends: "The LORD your God, He is God in heaven above and on earth beneath" (JOSH. 2:11).

But Rahab's hometown of Jericho was next in line for destruction. God had had enough — He was ready to judge its inhabitants for their centuries of blatant idolatry and moral corruption. Jericho would fall and the Israelites would claim it by the Lord and for the Lord. The spies were able to escape without being seen, thanks to Rahab's clever concealment. Because of her kindness to them and her faith in God, the spies gave her a scarlet cord and told her to put it in her window. They promised that when the Israeli army came back to attack the city, they would spare the house with the scarlet cord (and everyone inside). The army attacked Jericho, the walls came tumbling down, the city was set on fire, and no one survived — except Rahab and her entire household.

That scarlet cord was a priceless treasure to Rahab and her family because its very presence freed them from judgment and rescued them from death. God used a piece of red twine to separate the saved from the lost in Jericho that day. It wasn't the first time He used that strategy, and it wouldn't be the last. Many years before in Egypt, God used the blood of an unblemished lamb placed on the doorways of the Jewish homes to spare them from the plague of death. And many centuries later, God used the blood of an unblemished, innocent man placed on a cross to spare believers from the plague of death. It was no coincidence that Rahab's cord was scarlet red like blood — like the blood of an unblemished lamb, like the blood of Christ.

Here's the coolest part of the whole story: Rahab — you know, the innkeeper/prostitute — actually became an ancestor of Jesus. She ended up in the lineage of the Messiah, and she even made it into the Hall of Fame in Hebrews chapter 11. Now those are some nice things to have on your resume. Rahab eventually joined the Israelites and worshipped the one true God. Somewhere along the line she married Salmon and they had a son named Boaz. Boaz married Ruth (another awesome story there) and a few generations later King David came along... and eventually Jesus. You can read the genealogy in chapter 1 of Matthew, but the bottom line is this: no Rahab, no David. No David, no Jesus. No Jesus, no salvation for us. God can (and loves to) use the most unlikely people to bring His plans into action.

So Rahab lives on through the red strings on Ben Yahuda Street, but even she would have been saddened by the value people place on the symbol itself, instead of what the symbol represents. No amount of scarlet cords or crimson bracelets or red strings (or rabbit's feet or four-leaf clovers or guardian angel pins) can protect us from the plague of death. We only find salvation and deliverance when we find shelter under the one true scarlet treasure — the blood of Jesus Christ. "Therefore there is now no condemnation for those who are in Christ Jesus" (ROM. 8:1).

tf

Jesus said to them, "Therefore every scribe who has become a disciple of the kingdom of heaven is like a head of a household, who brings out of his treasure things new and old."

~Matthew 13:52

Something Old,
Something New

22

You may know (from my other books) that Jim and I were big movie buffs. One of our favorite films was *A Christmas Story*, and apparently we aren't alone since some television stations broadcast it as a twenty-four-hour marathon each year. Jim and I would even watch it throughout the year when we needed a fix and couldn't wait until December. If you've ever seen it, then you are well-acquainted with Ralphie, a nine-year-old boy on an obsessive campaign to acquire his greatest wish: "A Red Ryder 200-shot Carbine Action Air Rifle with a compass in the stock and this thing which tells time." (Must be spoken in high-speed mode for the full effect.) But the firm rebuttal from his parents, his teacher, and even Santa Claus was, "No. You'll shoot your eye out." Ralphie did eventually get his beloved Red Ryder BB gun — and he did almost shoot his eye out.

I love that movie and still enjoy watching it. I still laugh at every funny line. But it's never been the same watching it without Jim. And it's never been the same since my spiritual rebirth. Why? Because there's one particular line in the movie that bugs me now. It's the very last line of the movie when Ralphie (all grown up and narrating the story) says that the BB gun was "the greatest Christmas gift I *had* ever — or *would* ever — receive."

In my B.C. days, I never would have given that line a second thought. I thought it was endearing — a nice way to end the movie. And maybe you're thinking, "She's taking it too literally. It's just a fictional film." And maybe you're right. But it brings me back to the days when I, like Ralphie, considered something or someone other than Jesus to be the greatest treasure I had ever (or would ever) receive. Jim was a precious gift to me, along with many other earthly treasures. But I had yet to receive the greatest gift that can ever be given — the gift of eternal life.

Please don't misunderstand. I cherish the treasure of Jim and the very special memories of Christmases past with him. Celebrating holidays and birthdays and anniversaries without him is still a challenge. I'm certainly not saying that I should have loved Jim any less than I did. Of course not, and God would never have wanted or expected that. What I'm saying is that I should have loved God more. Like Ralphie, I loved the gift more than the Giver of the gift.

Christmases for me are much different now than they were in the days before I knew the Lord. I no longer put up a tree (which I always did before), but I do put up a nativity (which I never did before). My Christmas cards have manger scenes and Scripture verses on them — not snowflakes and Santa Claus. We now keep the family gifts to a minimum. Instead of exchanging, we each make donations to various Christian ministries. As we sit around the Christmas dinner table, we each take turns reading verses about the birth of Jesus from Luke chapter 2. And my new favorite Christmas movies? There are two, and they've both been around a while: First is the original Rankin-Bass production of *The Little Drummer Boy* — such primitive animation but such a profound message. I cannot make it through that movie without sobbing. If you're my age or older, you probably remember when major networks used to air *The Little Drummer Boy* every year. But once they started getting complaints that the Christian story was offensive to some people, they pulled it. My other favorite is *Charlie Brown Christmas*. Linus, dressed as a shepherd with his blanket as a prop, stands on a stage and tells the crowd what Christmas is really all about: he recites the passage from Luke 2:8-14, announcing that our Savior has been born. The networks still air *Charlie Brown*; and I wonder, for how much longer?

But I digress. The point I was trying to make is that my life before 9/11 contained many treasures, but my life after 9/11 has brought forth even more. I never would have believed that back then, but I know it for sure now. Jesus talked about how certain treasures appreciate in value with regard to the law and the prophets. In Mark chapter 13, Jesus tells a parable about a fishing net thrown into the sea. Its contents were pulled up and all the fish were sorted—good ones were kept, bad ones were tossed. That's what it'll be like on judgment day for the sorting of believers and unbelievers. Good ones will be kept and bad ones will be thrown into the lake of fire. Then Jesus finished the parable with these words: "Therefore every scribe who has become a disciple of the kingdom of heaven is like a head of a household, who brings out of his treasure things new and old" (MARK 13:52). In their divinely-inspired writings, Moses and the prophets had revealed God's law to the Jewish people, and the purpose of the law was to make them aware of their sin and their need to be forgiven. So Jesus was basically telling His disciples, "Do you get it? 'Cause if you guys understand that, then you've got some pretty valuable treasure." But the Old Testament laws and teachings did far more than identify sin. They pointed to the Messiah who would redeem the people from their sins. So Jesus was basically saying, "And if you also realize that I am that Messiah, then congratulations—you hit the jackpot!"

I often reflect on the Christmases with Jim and the traditions we enjoyed. Every year he would buy me a beautiful, new bathrobe and I would buy him the latest dive toy. We'd make a yearly

139

pilgrimage to Fortunoff's department store to buy a few new tree ornaments (they always had the biggest selection). We both loved using fancy wrapping paper and bows so there was a competition to see who could produce the most extravagantly wrapped gift. And as we opened our presents together on Christmas morning, Ralphie and his BB gun would be on television and hot mulled apple cider would be on the stove.

When I look back on my "old" life, I see countless treasures that the Lord gave me. Some of them are still here, some have been lost. But when I consider my new life with Christ, I see new treasures — and treasures yet to come — that have value far beyond words. On Christmas Eve, instead of wrapping presents, I wrap myself in prayer. On Christmas morning, instead of opening presents, I open the Bible. On Christmas and every day of the year, I thank God for sending us His son for the promise of treasure in heaven. Yes, I had some earthly riches before, and I still do now. But I hit the jackpot with Jesus.

·ţf·

"Go therefore and make disciples of all the nations, baptizing them in the name of the Father and the Son and the Holy Spirit, teaching them to observe all that I commanded you; and lo, I am with you always, even to the end of the age."

~Matthew 28:19-20

In the Footsteps of Paul— A Holy Land Travel Journal

In 1947, a remarkable and unprecedented discovery was made in caves near the shores of the Dead Sea in Israel. A precious treasure, hidden for two thousand years, was discovered when a Bedouin shepherd inadvertently came upon several large clay jars in a cave in Qumran. Inside the jars were over eight hundred ancient scrolls written between 250 B.C. and 68 A.D., including portions of every book in the Old Testament (except the book of Esther). The discovery of the "Dead Sea Scrolls" was profoundly significant because until then, the oldest Old Testament manuscript we had dated back to around 900 A.D. Now we have Old Testament scrolls that are over a thousand years older than that! Even more important was the comparison between the ancient scrolls and the current traditional Hebrew text, which was copied much later.

After twenty years of thorough research, it was concluded that there were "no major additions or omissions"7 and that there are "no important dislocations or disarrangement of the text."8 The occurrence of so few (and such insignificant) errors between the Dead Sea Scrolls and those of today's Old Testament clearly shows the painstaking care that was taken when biblical manuscripts were hand copied. Those scribes took their jobs very seriously! This assures us of the extraordinary accuracy and miraculous preservation of Scripture as long as we stick with reading a traditional, reputable translation (not a paraphrase) of the Bible. The Bible is unique treasure (there's no other book like it). It is versatile treasure (no other book has more usefulness). It is durable treasure (writings up to 3,500 years old). And it is sentimental treasure (it is indescribably special to those of us who live by it.)

What a gold mine was discovered inside those old pottery jars. You have to wonder what the Bedouin shepherd was doing around those caves, which are in the middle of nowhere. I've been to Qumran twice. It is made up of huge mountains of limestone rock landscaping the desert wilderness. From a distance, you can see the caves within the rocks but the access to the caves would be very difficult. I wonder if the Bedouin ever realized that God providentially used his trek in the wilderness to bring forth the evidence. I wonder if the Bedouin (who, like me, had probably never read a Bible before) ever became convinced of its accuracy and authority. I wonder if he had any clue at all what treasures he found in jars of clay.

As fascinating and significant and valuable as Biblical archaeology is, it should never be the basis for our trust in Scripture. The presence of a big discovery shouldn't prove our faith in the Bible, and its absence shouldn't shake our faith. It's easy and tempting to put all our confidence in the important discoveries that have been made and to put too little confidence in the divinity and authority of the Bible itself. Archaeology can expand our knowledge and understanding. It can confirm what we already know to be true. It can be a jewel in our faith, but it should never be the authority of our faith. That authority must come from the Truth, the whole Truth, and nothing but the Truth — from Jesus and the very Word of God.

144

In October 2006, I joined Pastor Fisher and his wife Carol on a biblical archaeology tour of Greece, Turkey, and Italy. On the "Footsteps of Paul" cruise, we visited the ancient ruins of many of the first-century cities where Paul had set up churches during his missionary journeys. While on the plane heading out to Athens where we would board our ship, I thought about how much God had changed my heart in the past five years. Before my conversion, I had absolutely no interest in Scripture or history or archaeology of any kind; now, biblical archaeology is one of my greatest passions. Back then, my idea of a dream vacation was scuba diving every day in the Caribbean. By no means did I have any desire to travel to a place highlighted by rocks and dirt and rubble and remains of ancient buildings. Yet there I was on that plane, reading up on the latest archaeological dig in Ephesus, knowing that just a few years ago I couldn't even pronounce Ephesus let alone tell you where it was. (For the record, EFF-eh-suss is in Turkey.)

So I thought I would share some of my travel experiences with you. If you read *A Teachable Faith*, then you'll recall I included my prayer journal from my first trip to Israel. Walking in the footsteps of Jesus truly made the Gospels come alive and deepened my relationship with Christ. Walking in the footsteps of Paul made the book of Acts and the Epistles come alive and gave me a greater appreciation for the joy and the challenges of the early church. I invite you now to walk with me and explore some of my favorite archaeological sites from biblical times. No shovels or hard hats necessary — come as you are and dig in.

October 27, 2006 — Athens, Greece

Athens was our first stop. We were scooped up at the airport and taken to the Acropolis before we ever saw our cruise ship. I hadn't eaten or slept much on the plane, so I was hungry and exhausted. But when we arrived at the Acropolis, I suddenly got a burst of energy.

When most people think of Greece, visions of the ancient Parthenon towering over the city of Athens comes to mind. And yes, it is impressive — along with all the other ancient ruins surrounding it — but my interest peaked when I saw the traditional site of the Areopagus. According to Acts 17:19, that's where Paul met with the Epicurean and Stoic philosophers and gave his sermon on Mars Hill. It's not a magnificent temple like the Parthenon. It's just a big, rocky hill with a stairway carved into the rock — nothing special to look at. It's not the site itself that intrigued me; it's what Paul said there.

> *Men of Athens, I observe that you are very religious in all respects. For while I was passing through and examining the objects of your worship, I also found an altar with this inscription, 'TO AN UNKNOWN GOD.' Therefore what you worship in ignorance, this I proclaim to you. The God who made the world and all things in it, since He is Lord of heaven and earth, does not dwell in temples made with hands...* (ACTS 17:22-24)

Paul's Greek audience was afraid of offending any of their gods, so just in case they had inadvertently missed one, they figured they were covered with that anonymous altar. Paul went on to tell them about their Creator and Maker of all things, about Jesus and the resurrection, and that life was not left to chance, as some Greeks believed. He told them that God would not judge them for worshiping false gods in their ignorance, but since they weren't ignorant anymore, they had no excuse. Some rejected Paul's claims, some weren't sure about it, and others were convinced and joined him before he moved on to Corinth.

I couldn't help but wonder — if I lived in Athens back then, would I have been like the typical Athenians who spent their time doing nothing but talk about the latest craze? What would I have thought about Paul's sermon? Would I have listened to him with an open mind, or would I have sneered and walked away? Would I have understood it? Would I have believed it?

Would I have been saved?

October 28, 2006 — Thessalonica and Berea (Greece)

The ruins at Thessalonica are mainly from the Byzantine era (third and fourth century), so not much is seen from the time of Paul. Our tour guide taught us how to recognize Byzantine structures: when the builders were constructing a wall, they would randomly throw in anything they could get their hands on. A typical wall would be made of red brick, chunks of marble, mortar, recycled stonework, pieces of pottery, even broken columns and capitals — all mixed together in an architectural hodgepodge. As if the builders said, "Whattaya got there? A wine goblet? That'll work. Throw it in." It reminded me of the church body: many different people with many different features, built on the same foundation for the same purpose.

When Paul was preaching in Thessalonica, some of the Jews were less than thrilled with his claims about Christ and they accused Paul of "turning the world upside down" (ACTS 17:6). No doubt that was not intended as a compliment, but it certainly could be taken as one. Paul and his team were quickly making Jesus a household name. The gospel was spreading like wildfire and the Jews couldn't stop it; some of the Thessalonians had already been converted. Paul started a church there but the Jewish leaders started a riot, so Paul hightailed it to Berea.

Berea was a lot bigger and busier than I expected it to be. It's

147

a bustling city and the only ancient ruins are a set of first-century steps that may have been the county seat. Paul was welcomed in Berea, where the Jews were "more noble-minded than those in Thessalonica, for they received the word with great eagerness, examining the Scriptures daily to see whether these things were so" (ACTS 17:11). Those Bereans were top-notch, first-class biblical private eyes. *Just the facts, ma'am.* They weren't about to simply take some ex-Pharisee's word for it, even if he did sound pretty convincing. They tested Paul's claims about Jesus against the Old Testament Messianic prophecies and they saw the truth. Upon close inspection of the gospel message, they recognized it was no cheap imitation. It was an authentic, priceless, one-of-a-kind gem. And as I sat on a bench in Berea waiting for our tour bus, I recalled an occasion when I needed to be a Berean...

One of my favorite movies is The Visual Bible's *Gospel of Matthew*, which is acted out literally word for word according to the New International Version of the Bible. Bruce Marchiano plays Jesus and personally I think he does a great job, even though no human can ever accurately play the role of God incarnate. My *Matthew* DVD is a valuable supplement to my Bible reading. It helps me relate to the stories and parables, helps me commit Scripture to memory, and it visually reinforces the teachings of Christ. And no, I am not being paid to say that.

Since I've watched *Matthew* so many times and I've become very familiar with it, I thought I'd move on to a different Gospel in movie form. I shopped online in the most famous cyber store named after large women warriors and found *The Gospel of John* on DVD. However, it was not produced by The Visual Bible. I ordered it anyway, without knowing any production details, hoping that John would be as biblically solid and sound as *Matthew* is. After watching it, I was shocked and disappointed.

I discovered that the movie was made by Mormons and some of the Scripture (which is based on the Good News paraphrase) has deviations pointing to the Mormon belief that we will all become gods one day. Also, it seems that the production company had been influenced by Dan Brown's ridiculous *Da Vinci Code* heresy that Jesus had a girlfriend. Mary Magdalene was portrayed as the thirteenth apostle, appearing in practically every scene, including the Last Supper. *That's* certainly not in Scripture. Nor were many other scenes in the movie.

Out of curiosity, I went back to the website and read all the customer reviews of John. Out of 189 reviews, 169 were rated with four or five-stars, many with glowingly-positive comments: "Faithful to the Scriptures..." "This was the real light..." "Unvarnished truth..." "An outstanding portrayal of Jesus..." and "Consider it art, or consider it truth — it is both." My stomach turned.

The digressions from the truth were easily missed by at least 169 viewers who are obviously not very familiar with the Bible and thought this movie was wonderful. (I have no doubt that if I had watched *John* in my B.C. days, I would've applauded along with them.) Only a handful of viewers who study the Scriptures picked up on the flaws and wrote comments about it. What is the harm, you might say, in using a little artistic license? The harm is that the producers of John are corrupting the very Word of God and misleading the gullible people who watch the movie. One day they will have to answer to God for that, and the consequences will be pretty severe. God gives us strong warnings against modifying the Scriptures. In Deuteronomy: "You shall not add to the Word which I command you, nor take from it" (DEUT. 4:2, NKJV). In Proverbs: "Every word of God is pure... Do not add to His words, lest He rebuke you, and you be found a liar" (PROV. 30:5-6, NKJV). In the book of Revelation — some of the final words in the Bible — placed there no doubt for the greatest impact: "I testify to everyone who hears the words of the prophecy of this book: if anyone adds to them, God will add to him the plagues which are written in this book; and if anyone takes away from the words of the book of this prophecy, God will take away his part from the tree of life and from the holy city..." (REV. 22:18-19). In other words, DON'T MESS WITH THE BOOK.

It's so important to test everything we see and hear against Scripture. I thank God for the clarity, accuracy, and accessibility of His Word, that I may use it to discern truth from fiction and wisdom from folly. I praise Him for giving us the Bereans as a strong example to follow. And until The Visual Bible makes a John movie, I'm gonna keep watching *Matthew*.

October 29, 2006 — Philippi, Greece

Our ship docked at the ancient Greek port city of Kavala (known as Neopolis in the Bible). It's an adorable little town with cute shops. Unfortunately, it was Sunday and the shops were all closed. Probably a good thing since I couldn't fit any more souvenirs in my luggage. Paul went through Neopolis on his way to Philippi (ACTS 16), and he would have taken the Via Egnatia (or Egnatian Way), which was the main road connecting Asia and Europe. Parts of the original Egnatian Way are still visible and intact. When we arrived at Philippi, I made a point of walking on it and getting some pictures. Now I can proudly say that I literally walked in the footsteps of Paul. Very cool.

Philippi has fascinating ruins. Some date back to the first century, like the awesome open-air theatre, which is still in remarkable condition, and a stone crypt that is thought to be the jail where Paul and Silas were held. Most of the other structures are from the later Byzantine era (third and fourth century, remember the hodgepodge of building materials), when Christianity had taken hold and left its mark in the form of crosses carved into columns and buildings. As we sat in the ancient theatre, an actor dressed like Paul came out onto the "stage" area and addressed us by reciting the entire book of Philippians word-for-word. His memory was exceptionally impressive, as was his delivery. His performance made our visit to Philippi even more special and helped us put all the pieces together.

Philippi was a wealthy city full of treasure — it had mountains of silver and gold mines. And since the Egnatian Way cut right through the town, the conditions for trading were ideal. Paul told the Philippian believers to "...work out your own salvation with fear and trembling" (PHIL. 2:12). The Greek word that Paul used for "work out" (which is *katergazomai*) specifically referred to the labor of miners. So the Philippians would have understood exactly what Paul was talking about. The precious metals were already there, buried deep within the mines. The Philippians just had to find the treasure and do something with it. God has given all of us special gifts and talents and skills; our job is to find out what they are and use them to glorify God.

That's what "working out your salvation" means. I cannot work *for* my salvation because it is a gift from God, by His grace. It's not about what I can do — it's all about what Jesus did. I cannot work for my salvation; instead, I must *work out* my salvation.

Have you ever looked through your high school graduation yearbook and realized that many of your classmates — who had so much potential — never did anything worthwhile with their lives? Have you ever given a Christmas present to a friend and then months or years later noticed that same present in their house, stuffed in a closet or buried on a shelf in their garage, obviously never used? As Christians, we are given gifts and opportunities to use those gifts. Not only the gift of eternal life, but also spiritual gifts. Jesus saved us. But not only does He save us *from* eternal punishment, He saves us *for* something. He has plans up His sleeve for every one of us. Our job is to work them out. Work out our salvation. Like a gold miner digging for precious metals.

As I said, the Philippian believers would have clearly understood what Paul was implying based on the strategic lingo he used. He was talking to people from a wealthy, gold-mining town, so he spoke their language. They knew the treasure of material riches, and they also knew the treasure of Christ. Yet, Paul also had to talk to them about anxiety and discontentment: "Be anxious for nothing, but in everything by prayer and supplication with thanksgiving, let your requests be made known to God. And the peace of God, which surpasses all comprehension, will guard your hearts and your minds in Christ Jesus" (PHIL. 4:6-7). The bottom line is that it doesn't matter how much wealth we have. It doesn't matter what millennia we're living in. It doesn't matter what burdens we carry or what treasures we bear. What matters is our recognition that the only way to finding joy and contentment is through Jesus Christ.

Here's the coolest thing about Philippi: God used this wealthy, Greco-Roman city as a major vehicle to spread the gospel throughout Europe, and He used two people (well, four, counting Paul and Silas) to get the ball rolling. One of them was Lydia, the "seller of purple fabrics" (ACTS 16:14). Financially, Lydia's lucrative profession would have kept her quite comfortable. But spiritually, she was missing something. She already worshipped the one true God; but after hearing Paul preach about Christ, she gained the honor of becoming first convert in Europe. She and her family were immediately baptized (in a babbling brook that is still in existence today — I got a picture of it). As a good businesswoman and a servant for Christ, she used her career to promote the spread of the gospel. When people came from the east and the west to buy her royal-purple fabrics, she'd no doubt tell them about the royalty of Jesus. She took the gifts that God had given her and she worked out her salvation.

The other significant person who helped spread Christianity to Europe was the jailer in Philippi where Paul and Silas had been imprisoned. We need to rewind to a previous incident:

A demon-possessed slave girl had been harassing Paul and Silas (well, the evil spirit was causing the trouble, not the girl herself). Her demonic fortune-telling ability was a tremendous source of income for her master, who was exploiting her unfortunate condition for personal gain. Needless to say, when Paul commanded the evil spirit to depart from her (which it did), the girl was overjoyed — but her master was furious. He accused Paul and Silas of influencing the people against Roman customs, and he got the mob worked up into such a racket that Paul and Silas were thrown into jail.

But that wasn't going to stop God and His perfect plan. He simply ordered an earthquake, which shook the foundation, loosened their chains, and set them free. The jailer, who knew he'd be held accountable for escaped prisoners, was just about to kill himself when Paul stopped him. The gospel message was presented, the jailer and his household joyfully accepted it, and they became the second family of converts in Europe.

God used a few people to accomplish a big purpose. Big doors open on little hinges, right? And He even turned the enemy's tactics against him. Satan's verbal abuse through the slave girl was meant for evil but God meant it for good. As I walked along the ancient stone path of the Egnatian Way... as I dropped a pebble into the babbling baptism brook... and as I peered into the remains of the rock-hewn prison cell, I thanked and praised God for using Paul and Silas and Lydia and the jailer. After all, the gospel had spread from Jerusalem to Turkey to Greece to Italy and the rest of Europe. Since I'm Italian, my early ancestors would have been influenced by the powerful message of salva-

153

tion through Christ. Eventually the gospel made its way to America, and I believed and received. Paul, Silas, Lydia and the jailer worked out their salvation and now you're reading a book about it.

And it all started in Philippi.

October 30, 2006 — Pergamum (Turkey)

Pergamum (or Pergamos, depending on your Bible translation) was one of the seven churches of Revelation, best known for the label Jesus gave it: "where Satan has his throne" (REV. 2:13, NIV). Jesus may have been referring to the cult of emperor worship that was prominent there. Or He could have meant the immorality that was rampant there. Or it could have been the fact that there were so many temples dedicated to different gods. One of those gods was Asklepios, the Greek god of healing and medicine. His symbol was a serpent — the same serpent icon used for the symbol of medicine today — and the early Christians would have recognized it as the figure of Satan in the Garden of Eden. In all likelihood, "Satan's throne" was a reference to a combination of all of the above. Jesus sternly warned the believers to get rid of the evil influences around them, lest they put themselves at high risk for serious judgment. The ruins that are left there today are proof that Jesus meant what He said and the people didn't listen.

Pergamum was the Mayo Clinic of the ancient world, and the serpent image of Asklepios was worshiped for any healings that took place. Sick people had to be interviewed and "accepted" into the temple of Asklepion, the way that students are accepted into college in our day. Seriously ill cases were denied treatment. After all, if they died, that would mean Asklepios wasn't the all-powerful god they thought he was. Hey, wouldn't want to discredit his deity or anything.

There are two things I will remember about Pergamum. First, as a pharmacist, I was reminded that I need to give glory where glory is due. Patients often thank me for my direction and guidance with their medications and ailments. They thank me for intervening when a potentially serious error could have occurred. They thank me for the role I play in getting their insurance company to cover their medication. Instead of taking all the credit and patting myself on the back, I should be transferring that gratitude to God. I should let my patients know that what I've done does not come from my own power — it is by God's healing power — and that it might be nice if they thanked God themselves.

One symbol of the medical profession is a serpent on a pole, also called the Rod of Asklepios. In the Bible, the serpent usually represents Satan. So, you might ask, why would the medical field ever use it to symbolize healing? Because it carries a much deeper (and far more palatable) meaning. In the book of Numbers, God used poisonous snakes to discipline the Israelites for their complaining and their unbelief, and many people died from being bitten. They realized their quandary was a result of their sins, so they repented and begged Moses to talk to God for them, which he did. God commanded Moses to make a bronze serpent and attach it to a pole so that those who are bitten could simply look at it and live (NUM. 21:6-9). But there was a much deeper meaning that the Messiah would one day bring. About fifteen centuries later, Jesus and Nicodemus were having a little talk, and Jesus brought up the snake event. "As Moses lifted up the serpent in the wilderness, even so must the Son of Man be lifted up; so that whoever believes will in Him have eternal life" (JOHN 3:14-15). Just as the Israelites were healed of their sickness by looking at the serpent on the pole, we can be saved today from the sickness of sin by looking to Jesus' death on the cross.

The other thing I'll remember about Pergamum is the tree. As our group was looking down a large cliff at the remains of the altar of Zeus, I turned around and saw a large tree behind us. It caught my attention because it had dozens of white tissues and white cloths tied around its branches. I asked our tour guide about it. He said, "It's a superstition. Some people come here and tie white cloths on the branches to ward off evil. Sometimes they are sick and the white cloth is their request for healing. And sometimes they just want to make a wish."

Have we learned *anything* in 2000 years???

November 1, 2006 — Ephesus (Turkey)

Pictures do it no justice. Ephesus is mind-boggling. When we got off our tour bus and stood at the entrance of the city, I was silenced. Ephesus is the largest archaeological excavation site in the world, and it's still ongoing. Located on the west coast of Turkey, it was an important seaport and trade center in the first century, and it was known for its pagan lifestyle. Paul eventually founded a church there, and Jesus lists it as one of the seven churches of Revelation. The ruins at Ephesus are phenomenal. They spread out for miles and many areas are still uncovered. I saw tops of ancient buildings peeking through the earth, covered by two thousand years of dirt and grass, begging to be revealed after being hidden for so long. It made me want to grab a shovel and start digging. The structures that have already been excavated are incredibly well-preserved and breathtaking, especially the landmark library building and the Great Theatre, which seated over fifty thousand people.

156

It was at the Great Theatre where the mob got rowdy after Paul rebuked them for worshipping the goddess Diana (aka Artemis) instead of the one true God. Read about it in Acts 19. Paul wasn't happy with the silversmiths who were making statues of Artemis. He told them that "gods made with hands are no gods at all." That didn't go over too well with the silversmiths, so they got the townspeople together in the theater and worked the crowd into a frenzy. Most of them didn't even have a clue why they had come together or why they were creating such a ruckus. "Great is Artemis of the Ephesians!" they all yelled, for two straight hours. I can only imagine how loud that must have been. The Great Theatre, built on the side of a mountain, has exceptional acoustics. Even if you're sitting in the nosebleed section, you can hear a whisper from the stage — no microphone necessary.

Diana (Artemis) was a goddess of the moon, wild animals, and fertility (don't ask me how they came up with *that* combination); and I must say, she was downright ugly and quite bizarre. Her statues and images portray her as having dozens of breasts — she was completely cluttered with them. (I can't help but wonder what she ever would've done if they had mammograms back then.) Nevertheless, to the Ephesians (and many pagans in that culture), Diana was a diva; so they built her the biggest, most elaborate, most magnificent temple in the ancient world. In fact, it was one of the seven wonders of the ancient world. Over 400 feet long, 220 feet wide, and 62 feet high, it had 127 massive pillars surrounding the sanctuary where the many-breasted image of Diana (who allegedly dropped from heaven) stood. It was the glory of Ephesus and people came from far and wide to see it.

When they laid the temple's foundation, the Ephesians brought their gold and silver jewelry to be melted and mixed among the groundwork, which they hoped would ensure the richness and longevity of the building. Their earrings and bracelets and necklaces actually became part of the floor, and it was

157

called a "foundation deposit." The pagan Ephesians were standing on temporary treasures for Diana. Meanwhile, the Christian Ephesians were standing on the eternal promises of God.

The temple of Diana was a center of controversy between pagans and early Christians. The theatre incident with Paul was one of many confrontations between the followers of Christ and those of Artemis. Fast forward to the twenty-first century: the promises of God still stand as strong as ever, but what about the temple of Diana? Destroyed. Demolished. There is one solitary, lonely pillar standing where the magnificent temple used to be. I think it's so cool how God allowed that one single column to remain. It couldn't be a more vivid reminder of where our most valuable treasure lies:

> For no man can lay a foundation other than the one which is laid, which is Jesus Christ. Now if any man builds on the foundation with gold, silver, precious stones, wood, hay, straw, each man's work will become evident; for the day will show it because it is to be revealed with fire, and the fire itself will test the quality of each man's work. (1 COR. 3:11-13)

Enough about the temple of Diana. Now let's talk about worms....

As I said before, Ephesus was a large seaport and an important trade center. Because of their prosperity, the pagan Ephesians were filthy rich and they flaunted everything they had. One of their characteristic trademarks was their clothing. They wore the equivalent of today's designer Fifth Avenue fashions and they earned the proud reputation of being "dressed like an Ephesian." They wore royal colors and elaborate styles and specialty fabrics — especially silk.

On our tour, we saw lots of mulberry trees in Ephesus, and we were told that they've been around for a long time. We were also told that in ancient times the silkworm industry was big in Ephesus. The silkworms would eat the leaves of the mulberry trees and consequently produce a fine, white silk, which was then dyed and made into those Fifth Avenue fashions. Mulberry tree leaves contain an uncommon substance (a unique treasure) that, once eaten by the worms, breaks down and produces exceptionally fine, rare silk.

So here's the life lesson: the quality of the silk was not dependent on the worm but on what the worm ate. In the same way, the quality of our spiritual life is not determined by our own existence; it is determined by *what we feed on*. Are we consistently starving ourselves with junk food like the Internet, television, and video games? Or are we continually nourishing our soul with prayer, Bible study, and Christian fellowship? The old proverb is correct: You are what you eat. Like those worms, I wanna eat the good stuff.

In the book of Revelation, Jesus gave Ephesus a mixed report card. He commended them for their perseverance and intolerance of sin and false teachers (REV. 2: 2-3). But He also rebuked them: "But I have this against you, that you have left your first love" (v. 4). The good news: from the time Paul first preached to the Ephesians to the time John wrote Revelation, they had radically progressed from being a predominantly pagan society to a predominantly Christian church body. The bad news: they eventually stopped eating mulberry trees and started eating thorn bushes. They lost their focus and priority. They were trying to please too many people and they compromised their high standards in the process. Being politically correct became more important than being biblically correct. If that sounds familiar, it should. It's the current condition of the United States of America. Our country was founded on Christian principles, but two hundred years later we've banned prayer in schools, mandated the teaching of evolution, and threatened to remove "One nation under God" from our Pledge of Allegiance and "In God We Trust" from our currency. We're eating thorn bushes instead of mulberry trees.

While walking along the streets of Ephesus, our guide showed us how the huge, ancient marble columns and sidewalks were held together by iron staples and mortar. It was fascinating to see how buildings were constructed without the technology we have today. So when Paul wrote these words to the Ephesian believers, they would have understood the parallel and the meaning behind it: "You... are of God's household, having been built on the foundation of the apostles and prophets, Christ Jesus Himself being the cornerstone, *in whom the whole building, being fitted together*, is growing into a holy temple in the Lord" (EPH. 2:19-21, emphasis mine).

Our own country was originally built on that same solid Christian foundation, but again, we see a much different story today. Like a romantic relationship, the excitement can quickly fade. The courtship starts out wonderfully passionate, but after a few years of marriage, familiarity breeds indifference and one spouse takes the other for granted. Ephesian believers had changed their diet and become spiritually malnourished. They lost the thrill of knowing Christ. They lost their appreciation for being forgiven. They had left their first love, and Jesus longed for them to return to Him. Our country has also changed its diet and left its first love, but Jesus stands ready to take us back if we restore our relationship with Him. Jesus warned the Ephesians, and He warns us as well: "Remember from where you have fallen, and repent and do the deeds you did at first; or else I am coming to you and will remove your lampstand out of its place — unless you repent" (REV. 2:5).

As I looked around at the vast ruins of Ephesus — its

160

beauty long gone — I prayed for our country. I prayed that the Lord would not remove His hand of blessing from us, for the sake of the faithful few who remain. I prayed we would heed His warning and take our sins as seriously as God does. I prayed for godly leaders and a national spiritual revival, the likes of which we've never seen before. I prayed we would return to our first love.

November 3, 2006 — Corinth, Greece

Two thousand years ago, it was a bustling Greek trade center for business and entertainment. Now it lies in ruins. At first glance Corinth looks like a dead city; but like most of the ancient Holy Land sites, it is very much alive with biblical history. Filled with first-century buildings and inscriptions that are mentioned in the Bible, it's a nugget of gold in an archaeologist's treasure chest.

Because of its ideal location near the canal connecting the Aegean Sea and the Ionian Sea, Corinth controlled the traffic in all four directions: on land (Greece to the north and south) and on sea (Turkey to the east and Rome to the west). Back in its day, Corinth had everything you could want in a cosmopolitan city. It was a major financial hub, so it was kind of like Wall Street in New York. It had sports, so it was kind of like Salt Lake City hosting the Olympics. It had entertainment, glitz, and glamour, so it was kind of like Beverly Hills or Hollywood. It had gambling and legalized prostitution, so it was kind of like Las Vegas. Somehow it even squeezed in a little religion among all the politics, recreation, and immorality, so it was kind of like... well, the general shape of our nation today. But we've already talked about that.

The pagan Corinthians served many gods and they had

twelve temples to prove it. They worshiped Aphrodite, whose temple employed a thousand "religious" prostitutes. The ruins of her temple can still be seen on top of a mountain called Acrocorinth. They also worshiped the god of medicine (Asklepios, same guy as the one in Pergamum), whom they hoped would heal their many sexually transmitted diseases. They worshiped Apollo (his temple is still there), Poseidon, Demeter, Kore, and many others. For the righteous few, they even had a token Jewish synagogue, which is mentioned in Acts 18 and can be seen in archaeological digs. A marble inscription found on a building clearly states "Synagogue of the Hebrews" (in Greek) and below it was a carving of three menorahs. Paul spent a year and a half in Corinth during his second missionary journey; and at that time, the leader of the synagogue (Crispus) was converted after hearing Paul's preaching about Christ (ACTS 18:8).

But in the beginning of his ministry, Paul's preaching didn't always have that same inspiring effect on all the Corinthian Jews. Many of them protested his teaching that Jesus was the long-awaited Messiah, and they took their grievances to Gallio, who was the Roman governor of Corinth. They wanted this crazy new fad called Christianity strictly prohibited, and they wanted Paul punished for introducing it. But instead of throwing Paul out of the city, Gallio threw their case out of court.

Gallio didn't dismiss the case as a result of becoming a believer himself; he dismissed it simply because he wanted nothing to do with judging the Jewish laws. It was a ruling of apathy, but a critical ruling nonetheless, since it protected Paul's right to preach Christ. Wait, it gets better: Gallio's brother was the famous philosopher Seneca. While Gallio was governing Corinth, Seneca was in Rome tutoring the emperor, Nero. Gallio's ruling to allow the preaching of the gospel formed the standard for other Roman judges. After all, what Roman judge would dare to challenge a verdict made by the brother of Nero's tutor? Gallio's decision to throw out Paul's case literally changed the course of history, since any other decision could have been a dead-end street for Paul's ministry. Instead, for the next decade, the gospel message was allowed to be proclaimed without fear of conflicting with Roman laws. And thanks to Corinth's ideal high-traffic location, the good news spread like wildfire throughout Europe and Asia.

The judgment seat (or *bema*) where Paul stood before Gallio (ACTS 18:12) is still there in Corinth today. The blue and white marble stonework is in remarkable condition — I took plenty of pictures. It's so awesome to see such a significant artifact from the Bible, especially since it serves as a landmark for the spread of Christianity. As I stood there facing the *bema*, I imagined Paul facing the Roman governor and waiting for his verdict. It boggles my mind how the decision of one man so greatly impacted history. I doubt that Roman Judge Gallio ever came to realize the role he played and how he was providentially used by the Supreme Judge of the Universe. Sadly, it seems that God had absolutely no value to Gallio. But amazingly, Gallio had tremendous value to God.

Back in Paul's day, being from Corinth wasn't exactly something you'd brag about. The immorality in the city gave the Corinthians such a bad reputation that there were slang terms to describe them. The verb "to Corinthianize" came to mean "to practice sexual immorality." A "Corinthian girl" was a term used for promiscuous women. With everything that was going on there in the first century, it's amazing that Paul was able to establish a church, and it's no wonder that he had a tough time keeping the church in line.

In 1 Corinthians 6:9-11 (NKJV), Paul reminded the new believers:

163

*Do you not know that the unrighteous will not in-
herit the kingdom of God? Do not be deceived.
Neither fornicators, nor idolators, nor adulterers,
nor homosexuals, nor sodomites, nor thieves, nor
the covetous, nor drunkards, nor revilers, nor ex-
tortioners will inherit the kingdom of God. And
such were some of you. But you were washed, but
you were sanctified, but you were justified in the
name of the Lord Jesus and by the Spirit of our
God.*

            I love the part
where Paul says, "And such were some of you." Because, yes, such
were some of us. But those lifestyles are correctable by the grace
of God and the cleansing power of Jesus. Paul saw firsthand how
God can radically transform lives. He saw "Corinthian girls" go
through extreme makeovers and become new creations — the
old is gone, the new has come (I COR. 5:17). He saw people who
had previously worshipped in pagan temples become people
whose own bodies were a "temple of the Holy Spirit" (I COR.
6:19). Paul and his new Christian converts walked around the
wicked and depraved city of Corinth confident that the Holy
Spirit would give them the power to resist the immorality surrounding them. "God is faithful, who will not allow you to be
tempted beyond what you are able, but with the temptation will
provide the way of escape also, so that you will be able to endure
it" (I COR. 10:13).

    Indeed, such were some of us. Indeed, such was I. But I was
washed... by the blood of Christ. I was sanctified... by the power
of the Holy Spirit. And I was justified... by the grace of God. So
whether we come from first-century Greece or twenty-first century New Jersey, God can reconstruct all of us. He can take our

164

rundown ruins and rebuild us into a stately residence fit for a King to dwell within us.

November 4, 2006 — Sailing from Greece to Italy

In Acts chapter 27, Luke writes about the famous storm that Paul encountered and the shipwreck that ensued. To refresh your memory: Paul was a prisoner being sent to Rome to appeal his case before Caesar. He was on a boat with 276 men on board, including soldiers and other prisoners. The weather started getting rough, the not-so-tiny ship was tossed. If not for prayer and the grace of God, they all would've been lost. They all would've been lost. (Go ahead, sing it.) We can determine from Scripture that it was late October or early November, which was a dangerous time to be out at sea. They encountered a hurricane-force storm and Paul firmly warned them that they should not continue their journey, but they ignored his travel advisory and kept going. As they were getting thrown around in the Adriatic Sea, Paul was visited by an angel of God who assured him that they'd make it to land safely, because God had some business for Paul to take care of in Rome. The boat was indeed shipwrecked off the island of Malta, but every passenger survived to tell about it.

Fast forward to November 3, 2006, as we neared the end of our Footsteps of Paul Tour. We were sailing from Corinth to Rome on a large, overnight ferry when *we* hit a bad storm, and our ship was rockin' and rollin' all night long. I was sitting in the lounge with the Fishers and a few other couples, and everyone was holding on to their coffee cups and trying to keep their balance. I looked outside at the pitch blackness through the large windows and saw the white foam of waves crashing on the windows. At first I thought it was neat. Then I realized that the dining room was on the top deck of the boat. *Hmm...those waves are really big.* I made my way inside my little cabin, climbed on the miniature bed, and curled up in fetal position. *Okay, so we're on the same body of water that Paul was on when he went to Rome. Our route is pretty much the same as Paul's was. We're traveling at the same time of the year as Paul did. And Paul's ship went down.* These were not comforting thoughts. Needless to say I did a whole lotta prayin' that night. Praise God, He got us to Rome safely just as He did for Paul. Unlike Paul's ship, we didn't have to throw cargo overboard (we got to keep our souvenirs). That excursion gave me a small indication of what Paul must have gone through in his treacherous storm. And he did not have the comforts and luxuries that our ferry had — and he did not have Dramamine. *Thank You, Lord, for Dramamine.*

I don't know about you, but it's easy to thank God for my blessings when it's smooth sailing, yet I have to make a conscious and deliberate effort to thank Him when it feels like my ship is sinking. I have to remind myself to praise Him for His power, His presence, and His promises. As I look back on some of the other big "storms" in my life — the struggles, the burdens, the heartaches — I see two things that resulted from all of them. First, they displayed God's power and His faithfulness. Second, they changed what I thought was important. My values changed. My priorities changed. My whole perspective changed. I cannot always predict those storms and I cannot always control them. But I can be prepared and equipped for them. Jesus finished His Sermon on the Mount with a powerful curtain call:

166

Everyone who hears these words of Mine and acts on them may be compared to a wise man who built his house on the rock. And the rain fell, and the floods came, and the winds blew and slammed against that house; and yet it did not fall, for it

had been founded on the rock. Everyone who hears
these words of Mine and does not act on them, will
be like a foolish man who built his house on the
sand. The rain fell, and the floods came, and the
winds blew and slammed against that house; and
it fell — and great was its fall (MATT. 7:24-27).

My house had been built on sinking sand. After the storm of September 11, it fell. But I asked God to reconstruct it for me, and He did. Since I've been built on the Rock of Christ, I came through a squall with cancer and I'm equipped for whatever climate changes life will bring in the future. I can face those storms because I trust the One who controls the weather, and I read His travel advisory every day. After the shipwreck comes the shelter. After the rain comes the rainbow. After the flood comes fulfillment. After the trial comes the treasure.

November 5, 2006 — Rome

Roma — you have to roll the "r" and go heavy on the first syllable — is just spectacular. It's one of my favorite cities in the world, and I'm not just saying that because I'm Italian. My previous trip to Roma was with my family a few years ago (you may have read about it in *Teachable*). Like that trip, I was thrilled to see plenty of normal toilets in Roma this time around. After finding (and refusing to experience) a few porcelain "holes in the floor" in Greece and Turkey, being in a modern city with luxury amenities (like an actual place to sit while relieving oneself) was a refreshing joy.

But how dare I complain about a few inconvenient bathroom facilities on our trip. When Paul was imprisoned in the horrific

167

Mamertime dungeon in Rome, he had no luxuries whatsoever. The dark, damp, gruesome prison cell is where Paul spent the remainder of his life before he was martyred just outside of Rome around 68 A.D. There's a hole in the ceiling (where they dropped the prisoners into the cell) and a hole in the floor (which I presumed was the toilet, but tradition claims that Peter was also held in this prison cell and that the hole in the floor was a spring that Peter miraculously created for baptisms.) Whatever. Those claims cannot be confirmed, so no one really knows what went on down there. Nevertheless, it was an awful, dark, dreary place and Paul, the great apostle, was chained inside of it. Many years before, Paul had written to the believers in Rome — encouraging words that still comfort us today: "The sufferings of this present time are not worthy to be compared with the glory that is to be revealed to us" (ROM. 8:18). As I stood inside the Mamertime prison, I wondered how many times that promise crossed Paul's mind, and how much joy and strength it must have given him. I know it does for me.

The Roman Forum was the commercial, religious, political, and legal center of the city. Its impressive ruins are so well preserved that I felt like I was walking back in time. One of the massive structures in the Forum is the Arch of Titus. It was erected in 81 A.D. in honor of Titus who destroyed the temple in Jerusalem in 70 A.D. (In case you haven't noticed, I downright refuse to conform to the modern, secular dating references of "C.E." and "B.C.E." Common Era and Before Common Era? Give me a break. This is yet another attempt to take God out of the equation and I will not tolerate it. But I digress...) Inside the arch is a dismal scene depicting the temple being ransacked. It shows a menorah, the table of the bread of presence, the sacred trumpets, and the exiled Jews being ruthlessly carried away by the Roman soldiers. The scene grieves my heart.

Titus and his army thought that they were taking away the Jews' greatest treasure as their spoil, but the Jewish Christians in Rome knew better. In Paul's letter to the Roman believers, he reminded them that it was not their lineage — whether Jew or Gentile — that would secure their salvation. He reminded them that it was not their good deeds — no matter how well they kept the Law — that would ensure their place in eternity. Paul stressed that their greatest treasure comes solely from the grace of God through personal faith in the resurrected Christ. So when the Jewish believers in Rome heard that their homeland Jerusalem had been ravaged by Titus and the future looked bleak for Israel, God's promises (through Paul) must have been so comforting to them. In spite of the devastation in Jerusalem and the dismal carvings on the Arch of Titus, the real treasure had not been lost. They still had the guarantee of eternal life. They still had God's Word. They still had Messiah Jesus. "Of Him and through Him and to Him are all things, to whom be glory forever. Amen" (ROM. 11:36, NKJV).

November 6, 2006

It was an exhausting two-week trip, but it was thrilling and enlightening and fascinating and unforgettable. On the long flight back home, I wrote to the Lord in my prayer journal, thanking Him for His grace and for giving me such a wonderful experience. Here is an excerpt from that journal...

Dearest Lord Jesus,

How I thank and praise You for Your abundant

grace and countless mercies on this trip... Thank You for keeping us all safe and healthy... and for the wonderful memories and the friendships that have formed over the past two weeks, Lord. What a joy it has been to get to know Bob and Anne Menzies... and Jane and Larry Wells... and Tricia and Robert Pollard... and Joann and Don Felker. Bless their hearts for the love they shared and the kindness they showed to me!

You have graciously allowed us to see many of the early churches of the New Testament, and I know it will change my Bible reading forever — now I can visualize these places as I read about them. It saddens me that most of the early churches have been destroyed, either by man or by the elements, but it's been two thousand years so I shouldn't be surprised. Anyway, I learned so much on this trip, Lord. I learned that, first of all, nothing lasts forever except Your love and our lives (if we put our trust in You). The things of this world will pass away, but we will never lose our salvation. All praise, glory, and honor to You, Yeshua!

I was also reminded of the consequences of our disobedience. You've taken me to four out of the seven churches of Revelation (Ephesus, Pergamum, Sardis and Smyrna) and they all lie in ruins — proof that You always do what You say You're going to do. You always give us a warning. You always give us a chance to repent. You always provide a way of escape. But we don't always listen to You. I pray for the church of this day — for

170

the body of believers — that we may all come to a deeper knowledge of what You expect from us, and that we would honor and serve You and follow Your Word.

Lord, I am absolutely amazed at how much ground Paul covered in his ministry, all without airplanes and cars and buses and cruise ships and high-speed ferries. Nothing stopped him; he just got up and went wherever You sent him and he never complained. I'm sorry for the times when I did complain, Lord. You always provided far beyond my needs, and I didn't always appreciate it. I know I need to take some lessons from Paul...

I always marvel at how you took the most unlikely person — a strongly anti-Christian Pharisee — and totally transformed him into one of your most dedicated servants. It's such an encouragement when I pray for those who don't know You, Lord. If You can change Paul's heart... and if You can change my heart... then You can change anyone, even the ones I think are hopelessly lost. I will never stop praying for them.

Thank You for showing us how You can use one person to change the course of history forever — and it was by Your power and his commitment to You. Through the trials, it was Your grace and Paul's perseverance. Through the uncertainties, it was Your guidance and Paul's trust in You. You made a great team, and Paul would be the first to give You all the glory and honor. And rightly so.

171

I pray, Lord, that I can follow in Paul's footsteps. I don't mean what I just did on this trip, I mean what I need to do in my life. I pray that I will take full advantage of every opportunity I am given to share Your love and Your plan of salvation with those who don't know You. I pray for the same endurance and focus that Paul had — as Your student, Your servant, and Your soldier. I pray that I will always share Paul's passion and desire to do Your will. And I pray that I will fight the good fight, finish the race, and keep the faith.

Yeshua, You are my greatest treasure and I love You.

tf

A Special Thanks

Before I even started writing this book, many people voluntarily made suggestions for its title. It clearly had to follow the same format as my previous books: A _____ Faith, and fill in the blank with a catchy adjective that begins with a *T*. There were some great ideas: A Tested Faith... A Transparent Faith... A Trusting Faith... A Timeless Faith... A Triumphant Faith. But none of them jump-started my heart enough to sit down and write a book based on those titles.

Until Wayne Smith, a friend and member of my church, read my first two books and then wrote this poem for me. As soon as I read the third stanza, my heart leaped and I knew immediately what the title for the third book would be. Thank you, Wayne!

> *I started so small*
> *You pushed me so far*
> *You gave me A Tempered Faith*
> *I knew so little*
> *You taught me so much*
> *You gave me A Teachable Faith*
> *Now I cherish You always*
> *Though You've always cherished me*
> *You've given me A Treasured Faith*

FAQs and QFAs

These are some of the Frequently Asked Questions (and my Quasi-Final Answers) that I receive through my website and at my speaking engagements. I'm grateful for your interest in my life and ministry, and I'm honored to share more of it with you!

1. *How is your family?*

    In my books, I've introduced you to the members of my immediate family. Readers often ask me how they're doing and what they're up to, so I think this would be the perfect opportunity to give you an update on everyone. A big thanks to all of you who inquire about their lives and pray for their well-being!

    My parents are doing fine. They've had a few health struggles, but, praise God, they are both in remarkably good shape. At eighty-one years old, Dad still plays golf and does fifty military-style pushups every morning. Sure hope I get his genetics. Mom still makes the best meatballs, homemade ravioli, and tapioca pudding, which is the reason why Dad has to do pushups every morning. They are both active in their church and since we live five blocks away from each other, I'm blessed to see them often.

My sister Maria used to travel with me on all my speaking engagements, but her job now prevents her from coming along to most events. As a home healthcare nurse, Maria has a ministry of her own. She gives people physical healing and she offers them spiritual hope. Her husband, Tom, was a schoolteacher for thirty-six years, but he's now enjoying retirement. Tom is a deacon in our church and is working closely with missionary friends in Italy to help raise their support. Maria and Tom are both very active in our church and will be traveling with me to Israel on a trip planned for April 2009. They have two grown sons: Kevin and Brian.

Kevin is a software engineer for a financial institution in Manhattan. He recently married Heidi, a brilliant and beautiful Egyptian Christian. Heidi brings a new depth of joy to our family, and we welcome her and thank God for blessing us with her love. My other nephew, Brian, recently spent a year in Costa Rica with Torchbearers Ministries. Brian is very musically gifted and plays in worship bands for two different churches.

As of the writing of this book (December 2008), my brother Anthony is doing well, all praise to God. When it was discovered that his brain tumor had returned, he began chemotherapy and his most recent MRI showed a reduction in the size of the tumor. He will continue chemo for another six months and will be re-evaluated at that time. We are so grateful for your prayers. Anthony's beautiful wife Carla, who is also a nurse, has been faithfully at Anthony's side through his health crisis. She lifts his spirit, encourages his heart, and cares for him with the love of Jesus.

My niece Tarah (Anthony's daughter) is growing up so quickly that I can hardly stand it. At the writing of this book, she is sixteen years old and she's taller than me. (Then again, most people are.) Tarah will be driving soon (be still my heart) and is starting to look into Christian colleges. Her passion and commitment to the Lord remains a strong source of inspiration to all of us.

2. *Do you still work as a pharmacist?*
    Yes, part time, in between traveling to speaking events and writing books and magazine articles. I am blessed with a supportive boss who allows me to be flexible with my schedule. After working there since 1989, the pharmacy is my home away from home — even though I only work a few hours a week!

3. *Do you visit Ground Zero?*
    I have not been there since the second anniversary of September 11. It is still a painful place for me to be and I prefer to visit places where I can recall happy memories of Jim.

4. *Do you still scuba dive?*
    No, not since Jim's underwater Memorial Dive in 2002, and I miss it terribly. Soon after that last dive is when I started writing and speaking regularly, so I have very little time and few opportunities to dive. However, I did recently visit our planet's most spectacular dive site, and a place where Jim and I always dreamed of going: the Great Barrier Reef in Australia. I didn't dive, but I snorkeled — and once again marveled at God's magnificent underwater creations.

5. *Any word on Jim's underwater memorial plaque?*
    Sadly, no. As many of you know, in 2002 a dive site was named after Jim in Grand Cayman (one of our favorite places to dive) and a bronze plaque in Jim's honor was mounted underwater on the reef. But on September 11, 2004, Hurricane Ivan barreled through Grand Cayman. The force of the storm and the surge of the seas either uprooted the plaque or buried it deep under the sandy bot-

tom. There have been several searches made, but to no avail — and I truly don't expect that it will ever show up. But I have peace about not seeing the plaque again. I trust that wherever it is, that's exactly where God wants it to be.

6. *Do you have any desire to remarry?*
After 9/11, my love for Jim was still so intense and I could not imagine being with anyone else. Once the ministry came about, my heart changed from a commitment to Jim to a commitment to Jesus. I cringe when I think about how lost I was and where I was headed if it were not for the love and grace of Christ, which is why I have consecrated my life to Him. He has my complete exclusivity. I have not dated since I lost Jim, nor do I plan to date. I am living by the 1 Corinthians 7:33-35 principle, where Paul says that those who are unmarried (or widowed) "have secured undistracted devotion to the Lord" because "their interests are not divided." All I know is this: if God wants another man in my life, He will have to change my heart. And yes, He's already done that a few times already. (In fact, God has molded and shaped my heart so many times in the past eight years that He probably has carpel-tunnel syndrome by now.) Thy will be done, Lord.

7. *How has your battle with breast cancer changed your ministry?*
God has used that experience to give me a new platform for outreach. As a breast cancer survivor, I can encourage and support other women in similar situations, showing them how to trust the Lord through their own health struggle. But God has not limited this ministry to outreach only for widows or cancer patients. Since we all go through adversity at some point in our lives, the message of God's faithfulness is intended for everyone.

8. *Do you have an agent who handles your ministry?*

Yes, His name is Jesus Christ. I also work with a Christian publicist and book marketer, but the Lord is ultimately in charge of my activities. He manages my schedule, He arranges my bookings, He accompanies me on my travels, and He deals with every detail so I don't have to! But if you'd like to get in touch with me directly, just visit my website: www.jennifersands.com. And if you'd like to get in touch with Jesus, just call out to Him in prayer. No appointment necessary — He's very accessible.

Endnotes

1. Ruth Caye Jones, "In Times Like These," 1944.

2. Terry Wilhelms, *Dear God, I Need to Talk to You*, Daily Devotional, Fort Worth, TX: Brownlow Publishing, 2007.

3. Terry Wilhelms, *Dear God, I Need to Talk to You*, Daily Devotional, Fort Worth, TX: Brownlow Publishing, 2007.

4. Billy Graham, *Hope for Each Day: Words of Wisdom and Faith, Daily Devotional*, Nashville: Thomas Nelson, 2006, June 1 entry.

5. Rick Hampson, "For Those Touched Most by 9/11, a Turning Point in Faith," *USA Today*, April 18, 2008.

6. Edward Bulwer-Lytton, *The Last Days of Pompeii*,1834.

7. Walter C. Kaiser, Jr. and Duane Garrett, *Archaeological Study Bible*, Grand Rapids, MI: Zondervan, 2006, p. 1491.

8. Joseph Free and Howard Vos, *Archaeology and Bible History*, revised edition, Grand Rapids, MI: Zondervan, 1992, p. 176.

The LORD bless you, and keep you;
The LORD make His face shine on you, and be gracious to you;
The LORD lift up His countenance on you, and give you peace.
(Numbers 6:24-25)

Acknowledgments

I have found that the Acknowledgments page is the most difficult part of a book to write. Attempts at thanking everyone who plays a significant role in my life (and in my books) has proven to cause mental paralysis. I've already been staring at a blank computer screen for forty-five minutes — there are simply not enough words in the English language to express what's in my heart, and anything I write seems so inadequate. So I realize I may sound trite or melodramatic or repetitive, but here I go.

To my precious family — Mom, Dad, Maria, Tom, Kevin, Heidi, Brian, Anthony, Carla, and Tarah: I thank my God for the treasure of each of you, every day! I rejoice in God's grace that I belong to this family of believers, and I marvel at how God uses our heartaches and health struggles to bring us closer to each other and closer to Him. I love you all dearly and I thank you for your encouragement, your strong examples, and for being the earthly glue that holds me together on this journey.

To Pastor Fisher: When you announced your retirement, my heart crashed to the ground and has remained there ever since. I cannot imagine our church without you, but I suppose you are indeed entitled to some rest after forty years of preaching! God uses certain people in our lives to teach us, guide us, and disciple us; and that is the role you have played in my life for the past six years. The impact you've had goes far beyond the four walls of our church, since I pass on what I learn through my books and speaking events. And the impact you've had will go far beyond this earth... it will go into eternity. May the Lord abundantly bless you and Carol as you begin this new chapter in your lives.

To my Laurelton Park church family: thank you for being such faithful prayer warriors, for bearing my burdens, and for "standing firm in one spirit, with one mind, striving together for the faith of the gospel" (PHIL. 1:27). I treasure every one of you in my heart and I praise God for bringing me into this church family. Thank you for always showing me the love of Christ and for your support and help with this ministry.

To my dear friends: You have walked with me through this journey and prayed with me through each roadblock... in fact, you all prayed this book into fruition! Thank you for always being there for me and enriching my life with your friendship. Special thanks to my dear sweet Veva Savage in Houston who continually reminds me that God has plans to give me (us) hope and a future.

None of this would be possible without my outstanding publishing team. I cannot thank you enough for the time and effort you put forth to edit, design, and launch these books. It is truly a joy and a blessing to work with each one of you, and I thank God for the gift of your friendship. To David Taylor, the Founder of The Olive Press: God providentially used you as a mighty vehicle to make an author and a speaker out of me! To Brian and Nina Taylor at Pneuma Books: I thank the Lord for the gifts of your knowledge, creativity, and wisdom. To my publicist, Sharon Farnell, and my marketer, Sharon Castlen: thanks for everything you do to help spread the gospel message through these books.

A special thanks to Michael Gomez for taking the photo that appears on the cover. I applaud how you use your gift for photography to serve the Lord. Thanks also to Lifeway's *Homelife* magazine for arranging that photo shoot and giving me permission to use the picture.

The cross on the cover of *Treasured* is the same one that appears on the cover of my other two books. It is a small cross (eight inches high) that was given to me soon after 9/11, and it was carved out of a steel girder from the World Trade Center. Rich DiPietro, I thank you again for taking a raw piece of wreckage and making something so beautiful and meaningful out of it.

To Dr. Pellegrino, Dr. Kaufman, and all the nurses, radiation technicians, and medical staff who treated me for breast cancer: I thank God for giving you the wisdom and skills to help me fight this... and I thank each of you for the kindness and gentle compassion you showed me.

To Rich Lau, my boss at the pharmacy and one of my dearest friends: thank you for being so flexible with my crazy schedule and for letting me continue to be part of the Briarmill team. Without your patience, help, and support, this ministry wouldn't be possible!

To the readers of *Tempered* and *Teachable*: many, many thanks to those of you who shared your thoughts after reading my previous chronicles. Your encouragement was fuel for the writing of this book!

To my Lord and Savior Jesus Christ... You have given me unfathomable riches and inexpressible joy, and it is all by Your grace and for Your glory. Please search my heart and see the love, gratitude, and adoration that I have for You and how I rejoice in the priceless treasure that we are to each other. Maranatha, Yeshua!

About the
Author

Jennifer Sands is a New Jersey native, where she graduated from Ocean County College with a degree in business. She subsequently earned her pharmacy degree from Philadelphia College of Pharmacy and is a member of Christian Pharmacists Fellowship International and Rho Chi Society, the National Honorary Pharmaceutical Organization.

Jennifer continues to work part-time as a pharmacist in New Jersey; however, the primary focus of her work is now writing and speaking to local, national, and international audiences on developing biblical growth and overcoming life's struggles through faith and trust in Christ.

BOOK I

A Tempered Faith

Experience Jennifer's gripping, firsthand account of the beginning of a young widow's journey. *A Tempered Faith* is the raw journal of Jennifer's emotional and spiritual battle to find footholds of faith in the midst of unthinkable tragedy. It is her candid story of love lost and, ultimately, new love found. Most of all, it is a joyful confirmation that what the Bible says is true: God is in control, He is listening, and He does love and care for us... even when the earthly evidence suggests otherwise.

US $17.95
ISBN-13: 978-0-9717330-7-7 / ISBN-10: 0-9717330-7-4

Available to the booktrade through all major wholesalers.
Distributed to the trade through STL/Faithworks
For more information visit: **www.jennifersands.com**

BOOK 2

A Teachable Faith

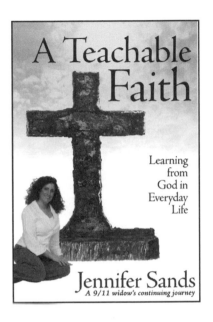

In her popular follow-up book, *A Teachable Faith*, Jennifer allows readers to have an intimate look at her spiritual growth as she adjusts to her new life with Christ and her new life without Jim. Grow along with Jennifer as she discovers the power of Scripture and realizes God's true purpose for her life. Learn from the powerful lessons that God taught Jennifer through everyday experiences. Joy, Trust, Peace, Strength, Wisdom, Patience, Change. It is all awaiting you… if you, too, can be teachable.

US $17.95
ISBN-13: 978-0-9767961-1-4 / ISBN-10: 0-9767961-1-2

Available to the booktrade through all major wholesalers.
Distributed to the trade through STL/Faithworks
For more information visit: **www.jennifersands.com**